YOUR BILLABLE LIFE

A LAW FIRM
SURVIVAL GUIDE
FOR NEW
ATTORNEYS

Bruce Dravis, Esq.

KAPLAN) PUBLISHING

New York

This publication is designed to provide accurate and authoritative information in regard to the subject matter covered. It is sold with the understanding
that the publisher is not engaged in rendering legal, accounting, or other
professional service. If legal advice or other expert assistance is required, the
services of a competent professional should be sought.

The opinions expressed in this book, unless otherwise expressly attributed,
are solely those of its author. The contents of the book are the sole responsibility of the author and are not the opinions, statements, or policies of the
author's law firm or its partners.

© 2008 Bruce Dravis

Published by Kaplan Publishing, a division of Kaplan, Inc.
1 Liberty Plaza, 24th Floor
New York, NY 10006

All rights reserved. The text of this publication, or any part thereof, may not
be reproduced in any manner whatsoever without written permission from
the publisher.

Printed in the United States of America

Library of Congress Cataloging-in-Publication Data

Dravis, Bruce F.
    Your billable life : a law firm survival guide for new attorneys/Bruce F. Dravis.
        p. cm.
    Includes index.
    ISBN 978-1-4277-9818-3
1. Practice of law–United States. 2. Law partnership–United States.
3. Lawyers–United States. I. Title.
    KF300.D73 2008
    340.023'73–dc22   2008039304

10 9 8 7 6 5 4 3 2 1

ISBN-13: 978-1-4277-9818-3

Kaplan Publishing books are available at special quantity discounts to
use for sales promotions, employee premiums, or educational purposes.
Please email our Special Sales Department to order or for more information at kaplanpublishing@kaplan.com, or write to Kaplan Publishing,
1 Liberty Plaza, 24th Floor, New York, NY 10006.

For Liane

Contents

Preface

Throughout this book there is statistical or numerical information that is presented about the present-day size of law firms and the salaries and working conditions, associates face including billable hour minimum figures. I have relied on a number of sources for such material, and have generally cited specific sources for unique information or direct quotations.

In other cases, and in particular with respect to the discussions of industry trends, I have relied primarily on the following recent and excellent source materials. I recommend to readers for additional insight and further elaboration on information that I have only excerpted or summarized in this book:

- "The Elastic Tournament: The Second Big Transformation of the Legal Industry," by Marc S. Galanter and William D. Henderson, 60 *Stanford Law Review,* 102 (April 2008) ("Tournament")
- "Overview of the Professional Services Industry and the Legal Profession," a report provided to the Alfred P. Sloan Foundation by the Harvard Law School Center on Lawyers and the Professional Services Industry, by Sean Williams, JD,

Research Fellow and David Nersessian, JD, PhD, Executive Director (2007) ("Sloan Report")

- "After the JD," NALP Foundation for Law Career Research and Education and American Bar Foundation (2004)
- "How Much Do Associates Have to Work?" *NALP Bulletin* (2007)
- "Law School Debt Among New Lawyers," by Gita Z. Wilder (2007)

Acknowledgments

I want to thank Kelli Christiansen, for having identified the project and gotten me involved, and the editors, Josh Martino and Michael Sprague, for their excellent help.

Introduction

At the very beginning of your legal career in a law firm, you are a blank slate. You have no accumulated legal work history, although you probably have work experience from some other venue prior to joining the law firm. You have strong grades from a quality school and you have been an excellent student your entire life. You are accustomed to success. You are accustomed to making accurate judgments. You are accustomed to performing at a very high level. So why are your odds of making partner at the law firm you join so low?

This is not intended to be discouraging, but to be realistic. You may make partner in the firm you join after law school, but there are a lot of associates who do not, and we are talking in all cases about highly intelligent, talented, focused individuals.

Some of it is the luck of the draw. You might wind up working with a partner whose practice is only moderately successful, or you might work in a segment of the legal market that has low or no growth, while your peers may get lucky doing work in the next big thing. You might wind up working with a partner who has his own individual advancement within the firm at heart, and who treats your training, development, or success as a secondary matter. In fact, I guarantee you will work with a partner who will treat your success as secondary. You are going to have to own your own career and track how it is going and make decisions on how to make it better.

The goal of this book is to provide you with an idea of what to expect in law firm practice and how to handle the challenges you will encounter. The book is not a road map. It is more like one of those U.S. Forest Service contour maps that shows you where the hills and ravines are located, but not the specific paths, which you will have to discover yourself.

TO GET WHAT YOU WANT, KNOW WHAT YOU WANT

How will you know if you have achieved success?

This book assumes that you will make correct ethical and moral judgments, and so it is not about choices that are "right" in an ethical sense, but in the sense of being effective at promoting your career success.

To analogize to the world of professional financial advisors and investors, finding out that you have blind spots in your investment decision making has direct dollar costs that the universe imposes without favoritism or judgment. If you make a bad choice, you lose money. If you stay with a bad choice, you lose more money. The universe is not imposing a punishment; there is no moral judgment at work. There are just choices that work profitably and choices that do not.

When you think about your career, or any life choice more significant than which kind of coffee to order at Starbucks, you face the same universal imperative as an investor. Some choices succeed and some do not. You have the same 24 hours in a day as everyone else. The key question, in light of who you are, your personal history, talents, and personal goals, is what way of spending them will be best for you?

You have a set of skills and talents, you have a life story, and you have personal and family relationships—all of which represent tangible and intangible assets that are unique to you. None of these elements dictate what choices you are required to make. They are the resources you get to use to make the best of the choices that you make.

If you are reading this book, you are probably a law student or a recent law grad, and you are starting or considering a career in a law firm. There are plenty of venues other than law firms for attorneys to use law degrees. There are large numbers of government jobs, whether federal, state, or municipal; there are jobs in the judiciary, in administrative positions, or as prosecutors or public defenders. There are public interest firms, there are lobbying firms, there are think tanks, and there are teaching positions. There are plenty of jobs in the private sector, and often law students take joint MBA degrees in order to pursue positions with companies that want people with legal backgrounds to do financial or operational jobs. There is also solo practice.

This book is not about making non–law firm choices, but such alternative career choices exist in the law. In light of your other life choices and your goals, you should be willing to examine the fundamental choice about whether to enter into private practice in a law firm.

A career in law can provide a solid income and possibly even wealth. It can provide intellectual challenge. It can provide the opportunity to work with talented professionals as colleagues and as clients. It can be a chance to advance the cause of justice, to ensure that society works smoothly to help make the world better. You may find any of these reasons to be valuable and sustaining long-term motivations to pursue your legal career.

Coming from school, with the high cost of legal education, you may have a short-term goal of paying off student loans.

As this book is intended to be practical rather than theoretical or philosophical, the suggestion that you keep in mind your personal goals is intended to be pragmatic. Knowing your personal goals will help you understand what you are attempting to do with the degree you spent so much money to get. Knowing your goals gives you a baseline from which to measure whether you are making progress. Having a direction, even if the direction changes, can help lend structure to the career choices that you make.

Not everyone does, or can, measure progress toward life goals, either day by day or even year by year, but making the effort will help you have perspective on what you are doing.

The good news is that most attorneys who self-select to be in law firm practice are happy with that choice. [See "After the JD," a joint publication of the NALP Foundation for Law Career Research and Education and American Bar Foundation (2004), Page 47.]

HOW TO READ THIS BOOK

A lot of this book will seem like basic instructions on how to behave in an office, and many of the recommendations may seem so commonsense as to be little more than a restatement of the obvious. I know that. There are going to be parts of this book that you will read and think, "Only an idiot would do that." Trust me. No matter how commonplace the recommendations are or how obvious the advice seems, you can be sure that someone somewhere has done it the other way, to the detriment of both attorney and client.

This book will discuss what you should expect to see or consider in law firm practice. Not all law firms are the same, but they share similar characteristics. Some of the specific topics covered are the following:

- What you should do
- What you should not do
- What you should expect to learn
- What life and work issues you should expect to face

To tie these discussions about law firm life to your goals, you should keep these questions in mind as you read the book:

- What motivates you: Money? Status? Competition? Achievement?
- Law firm practice, particularly in the largest law firms in major cities that have national and international practices, can provide significant professional status and high pay, in a highly competitive and achievement-oriented environment.
- Not all law students qualify to get positions in those firms, and not all law students who qualify for such positions want them. As discussed in this book, not all associates who join such firms stay with these firms, or stay with large firm practice, or become partners when they stay.
- For attorneys who join regional or small law firms, the considerations are similar. The legal profession, generally, has a certain level of social status and ultimately is white-collar work that tends to pay reasonably well, even in firms that do not represent Fortune 500 clients.
- Whatever your primary motivator is, keep in mind as you read the discussions in this book that you should evaluate whether the things that make you enthusiastic are consistent with the descriptions of law firm practice.

- How important is money to you? The firms that pay the most money will make the highest demands on your time and your dedication. You may find that the money is highly desirable, but the demands associated with making the money are not.

- Can you balance work with the time you want to spend with family and friends? Law jobs in any environment will require significant dedication of time. All law firms involve hard work, although the amount can vary by firm. If you are a new associate or a summer clerk, ask the partners or associates for some war stories about late nights or long weekends spent on projects, and whether those events are occasional or routine. People will tell you if you ask. You can then incorporate those answers into your thinking about your goals.

- What is your personality? There is no single personality type that is required in order to thrive in the law firm environment. That said, if you are indecisive, dogmatic, or arrogant, you may find that your personality does not give you an advantage in the law firm environment.

- How do you resolve conflicting demands? You will be required to resolve conflicts in your law career. You may be involved in litigation, in which the entire activity is conflict related. Transactional law involves negotiations to resolve differences among parties in how a deal will be conducted and concluded. Within the law firm, you will be required to balance demands to produce work for different partners. You will also be required to reconcile demands on your time by the job and by your family.

- If you are not already good at mediating and resolving conflicts, you should prepare to get better at it.
- Will you be able to find satisfaction in your work? Some of the initial work any associate does will be similar to what you did in law school. There are plenty of research assignments, plenty of opportunities to write on the status of the law, and typically little in the way of direct client service. Over time, some of the assignments can seem rote, but it will be important in terms of maintaining motivation and job satisfaction to treat the early portion of your legal career as an apprenticeship in which you are learning the practice and looking for opportunities to expand your skills.

BE PREPARED TO WORK HARD

As of 2008, the cost of three years of law school—just tuition—was running about $120,000 for students at Harvard, Yale, or Stanford. Other law schools have tuition at similar lofty levels. For students who have to borrow, or have their parents foot the bills for their educations, that represents a very significant investment of money—not to mention the three years of living expenses.

When I was a first-year associate, a partner with whom I worked was reflecting on his law school years as the "good old days." Having just served as editor of a law journal and otherwise working hard during law school, I thought he was crazy. Now I think he was right.

If you have a huge student loan to repay, private sector work can look very attractive. Starting annual salaries for the leading law firms in New York, Chicago, and other leading cities is about $160,000. These salaries go a long way toward getting the loans paid off, although these cities are also expensive places to live. There may even be the chance to have something left over to have a life, buy a house, get started on a family, or other goals that you might want to pursue.

Depending on your life circumstances, you might not approach the choice of working in a law firm with any enthusiasm or depth of caring. It may have been a default choice, the thing that you saw other classmates doing.

If you lack enthusiasm for working in a law firm, you should develop it before you start or find ways to develop it quickly once you start. You will need to be motivated and enthusiastic in order to tackle the work that needs to be done if you are going to succeed in a law firm. Law firm practice will require significant time commitment and significant emotional commitment.

You need to be able to make that commitment or last long enough to develop it.

Lots of associates get washed out at law firms. There are many talented and intelligent attorneys who find that the environment and demands of law firms are not for them. Law firms do not reward good people for being good. They reward good people (and sometimes even people who are sort of rotten) for working hard and delivering products and services that the clients need, within the time frame that the clients need them.

You do not have to think of yourself as a hard worker, as long as you work hard. Many of the hardest workers just work and never think about whether they are working hard or not; they just put in the hours. There is inevitably a commitment of time that is needed in order to generate the quality and amount of work that is required.

There is a considerable amount of literature on how the attitudes of baby boomers differ from the attitudes of their children. The difference is not characterized as an unwillingness to work by the newer generation, but as a desire to work with an advance understanding of where the toil ultimately is taking them. Also, the newer generation is said to have the objective of keeping work and other elements of life in balance, rather than believing that in some distant and unknown future where they will hold assets sufficient to buy their leisure.

Fine. Most of the time, law firms do not care whether the work gets done at midnight after the kids are in bed, or in the morning, or in the office—although you need face time in the office so that you can become a known quantity to your partners and fellow associates. In the end, if the client does not get the work on time, or if the quality is not there when the work is delivered, then the marketplace will administer its judgment: the clients will stop giving the partners work, and the partners will stop giving you work. You will be in a constant balancing act, dealing with the competing demands of lovers, spouses, friends, family, and children, and finding time for your own personal interests and the needs of partners and clients.

Be ready for it.

Just because millions of people have gone through the same problem does not mean that when it comes your turn you will be any good at it.

How you deal with it will be up to you.

Chapter 1

What Law School
Taught You

(and Didn't)

L AW SCHOOL INVOLVES A three-year study of the field,
starting typically with the building-block courses
that teach concepts that are key to all other aspects of
legal analysis and practice:

- Property, which teaches basic concepts of ownership, identification of ownership, and transfer of
ownership
- Contracts, which relates to the formation of contracts, the elements of contracts, and the rem-
edies for breaches of contracts
- Torts, which teaches the elements of what is and
is not a harm for which the law permits recovery

1

and under what circumstances, and the concepts
of social duties to prevent harm
- Civil procedure, which teaches how cases are
brought to and handled in court
- Criminal law, which teaches the elements of
crimes, the proof of the elements of crimes, and
defenses to criminal charges

After the first year in law school, the additional
course work builds on these concepts to provide students with understanding of specific areas, such as
evidence, tax, corporate and securities, or environmental law.

Law school work relies heavily on students reading
cases, learning how to find the holding of the court in
a case, and learning from the cases both the general
principles of law and how those principles are applied
in the specific factual circumstances of the particular
case.

Case reading provides useful behavior modeling for
the work of a lawyer by requireing law students to see
repeatedly how a court handles the process of identifying key facts, setting out the legal principles involved in
the dispute, and applying those principles to the facts
at hand in order to present a conclusion.

The process of "thinking like a lawyer" is one of
accretion, in which you have learned over time how
to identify, sort, rank, and apply salient facts that are
key to making a decision on what is and is not within
the law.

In practice, you will be called upon constantly to learn the facts and to apply the legal principles relevant to the matter at hand.

However, your clients will not always come to you with their questions conveniently labeled "contract" or "tort" the way matters were presented in law school. Clients will bring a set of messy facts, with the expectation that you will find the relevant ones and help them understand the law that should govern the situation, in the hope that your help will generate the result they desire.

A matter might start out looking like a contract dispute, then veer off into tort if the facts develop that a third party has conducted a tortious interference with a contract. A claim that you intend to assert might require the proof of multiple legal elements, and as you dig into the facts, you may discover that not all the elements are met, changing the analysis of the issues on which claims can be brought or defenses can be maintained.

There is nothing more constant in law than the need to discover additional facts in order to make the case or make sure that there is not a defense or superior claim. Law school entails reading and more reading, and analysis and more analysis, and the process of learning to truly think like a lawyer.

All of that law school training is required for you to work in a law firm; but at the same time, law school training does not prepare you for what you will encounter in practice. Attending law school is a necessary, but not sufficient, precondition to conducting the practice of law in a law firm.

WHAT YOU SHOULD HAVE LEARNED

In the American system, learning to read cases is tremendously important. Many areas of law require nuanced applications of legal principles to facts presented by the client. There are frequently questions that clients pose that do not fit neatly within the four corners of the law, but require you to reason by analogy: If the client's facts are most like this case, then this same principle should apply to my situation.

The narrowness of court holdings is an important concept. The essence of law practice is discerning the applicability to your client's situation of a precedent that is based on a similar, but not exactly matching, set of facts. As an attorney, you want to draw the right analogies and provide your client with the right result.

Not all aspects of law are governed by case law. Many areas of practice are governed by statutes or by specific regulations, which can be significantly detailed. The specificity of the rules notwithstanding, not all answers to all questions will be found within the rules. Once you advise a client about how to comply with the regulations, you are in essence projecting into the future what the result of a court dispute would be if the course you recommend is challenged by a third party or by regulatory authorities.

Evidence is not a typical first-year course, but the concepts of what is and is not relevant, and what is and is not probative, are incredibly important aspects of working in law. Ultimately, evidence questions are bound up with the facts. You will deal not only with the question of determining what the facts are, but also the issue of how, if challenged, you would demonstrate what the facts are.

Each document that you prepare is part of a chain of evidence. A deed is evidence of the name of the record owner of a property, of the boundaries of that property, and of the restrictions that govern that property. The deed is not a complete record of all the facts relevant to the property; zoning ordinances can affect the property, and the information would not be within the four corners of the deed. The creation of an easement by ongoing course of action, a matter of facts that would have to be demonstrated to the court, would not be within the four corners of the deed. But the deed would be the powerful evidence that you would use to begin determining a party's legal right respecting a parcel of land.

IN LAW SCHOOL, YOU GET GRADES; IN LIFE, YOU DON'T

In all likelihood, you have had some work experience in your life, rather than having been only a student. Nonetheless, the key shaping factor in your law school life has been your success as a student. The job of a student is to absorb the lessons that the teacher has been attempting to impart and to respond either in the form of a test or a paper to the professor's inquiries as to what has been learned. As a student, you are set the task of learning what the professor has to say about a subject. At the end of the course you are provided feedback, quantified in the form of a grade, as to the professor's impression of what you have in fact learned—however arbitrary or incomplete the testing and grading formats may be for any course.

Outside of law school, the model is different. You must still learn, you must still demonstrate what you have learned, and you will still get feedback. However, in a law firm the form of the learning, the demonstration of knowledge, and the feedback are all very different from the structured setting of law school.

Learning the Law in Practice

You must learn the relevant law to the question at hand. Unlike the law school setting, where the professor is presenting the relevant law to you in order for you to learn it, the partner providing you work in the law firm setting may or may not know all of the specific elements of the law that you will be required to learn. Part of your job in any given project may be to help the partner learn what the law is—what new cases have affected the prior interpretations of a statute or regulation, what new regulations have been adopted, and whether new statutory requirements have been enacted.

For any given project, however, you may not be certain that you have all of the relevant law unless you are certain that you have all of the relevant facts. Accordingly, you may find yourself in an iterative process, starting with what you think are the relevant facts, then finding the law, and learning whether there are additional facts that you need to incorporate into your analysis. After you obtain those additional facts, you will need to find the law relevant to those facts. In some cases, you will make assumptions about alternative versions of the facts and conduct an analysis along the varying outcomes.

What you intend to learn about the relevant law can vary depending on whether you are attempting to review past actions or provide advice on future behavior.

For example, if you are trying to help a company develop an approach to complying with an employment law or an environmental law, you might have to consider what the legal outcomes would be depending on what kind of conduct the company decided to adopt. In other words, you are looking forward in time and trying to help the client avoid legal problems. In that case, the facts relevant to the application of the law, such as the company's behavior or the company's adoption of a relevant policy, would not yet have come into being.

The client may—for reasons having to do with cost, existing installed facilities, or the predilections of the management—adopt a very cautious approach to legal compliance to ensure that there is never a question of whether the client is behaving in a way consistent with the law. Alternatively, the client might adopt an approach that involves an interpretation of the law in a "gray area" that leaves the potential for future challenge by third parties or regulators.

In that regard, it is critical to note that there is a difference between a client who elects a course of action where the legal outcome is not certain versus a client who wants your help in adopting an approach that clearly falls outside settled law; in the latter case, you have to tell the client that you are not the right person to provide legal advice.

In a litigation context, you are looking backward in time. You are trying to determine whether the specific facts support or do not support a cause of action that you are trying to bring or a defense that you are trying to assert.

Sometimes you will not know the facts, or you will be missing one key factual element. In those cases, you would consider the legal outcomes in the alternative— if the client did A, you get this result; if the client did B, the result is something else. Thereafter, you will seek the facts to learn which outcome will be supported by the evidence.

Demonstrating Knowledge in Practice

In law practice, you will not be given a date for the test, time to prepare for it, or a course outline to let you know what the questions will be on the test.

You will get questions and follow-on questions from the partner. You will get a document to prepare, or a memo to write. You will be asked follow-on questions in front of the client or other partners. You will be put on the spot in a series of pop quizzes on topics that may be related to the one that you actually prepared for, but are not exactly what you were prepared to answer.

After you have articulated a legal principle relevant to a singular set of facts, you may be presented with a set of alternate facts to demonstrate the kind of analysis that you can do or to test where the boundaries of the law are drawn.

In other words, just answering the question will not be enough since there will certainly be follow-on questions, questions on alternatives, and questions on related topics.

The form of your demonstration of knowledge could be a legal memo, which would be similar to a lot of writings you would have prepared for law school. Or it could take the form of preparing an advisory letter to a client or a contract embodying the principles that you have reviewed.

It will not be enough simply to get the legal issues right. It will also be necessary to articulate your knowledge crisply and accurately.

In a test for a law professor, where the professor knows what the answer should be, you might get some credit for being substantially right even if your answer is not precisely phrased. In practice, precision of expression will be necessary at all times. As a first-year associate, I once dealt with a partner who would correct my sentences—in oral reports, as I was saying them.

The experience of being corrected constantly to achieve precision is part of the associate experience, and you should absorb this teaching as it occurs.

What You Get Instead of Grades

Law school provides highly structured feedback in the form of grades. Legal practice will not provide you with the same kind of feedback:

- You will not be told directly if your memo on a point of law is graded with an A, or a C, or an F.
- Depending on when the partner is able to review the material you have prepared, you may or may not get an immediate response to your work.
- The needs of the client may change, so what you prepared may be superseded by a new requirement, and you may end up doing more than one version of the same document, altered from the original request to reflect the refined questions.
- Your single issue may be part of a larger set of questions and may turn out to be irrelevant in light of other facts or legal analysis that is developed.

In all of these cases, you may get limited feedback, only partial feedback, or feedback that it is not immediate.

If you have done a job that is so overwhelmingly good and thorough that you have anticipated every conceivable question that the partner might theoretically have asked you on the topic or any related topic, you might be told that you did an excellent job. Or you might be told that you exceeded the question's scope and the client's needs and that the partner will have to write off some of your time. In other words, you will have to be thorough, but it may not always turn out to be a virtue.

You will be told in a general way, but not necessarily in a structured way, how good the product is. The "After the JD" survey of associates shows that the area of least satisfaction for associates in law firms is the feedback and evaluation process.

Even if immediate and accurate feedback would be valuable to your development as an associate, the partners in the firm may not provide it, for various reasons. For one thing, law firms are focused on their deliveries to their clients and not necessarily on their internal processes, including the internal development and evaluation of personnel. Dollars spent on development are worthwhile and firms spend them, but associates leave. They take the training and go somewhere else.

Partners do not get paid to develop associates. They get paid to deliver work to clients. However necessary to the ultimate success of the firm the development of quality associates is, associate development is not the primary mission of the firm—service to clients is.

Associates typically get evaluations at least annually to help them understand where they need to improve and how they are doing relative to the expected stage of development for someone at their number of years out of law school. The partners will also have a generalized sense or perhaps a quantified sense of how the associates rank compared to one another, but this information will not necessarily be shared with associates. This is in part because relative associate rankings can change from year to year, particularly in early years, and in part because offering that sort of information could be the source of more problems than solutions.

Continuing to provide work assignments to an associate will be the sincerest form of enthusiasm that a partner can show. A partner may be obligated not to monopolize an associate, so the absence of additional work from a partner may not be a sign of any unhappiness; it may reflect the internal firm dynamics of letting your work be known by multiple partners.

You will want to have shown your work to multiple partners and have multiple sources within the firm to verify the quality of your work. If you work with only one partner, you will have a risk that the particular partner may not carry the day for you when the time comes for the partnership decision.

Working for only one partner may provide you with an opportunity to know a client or practice area in depth and to develop real expertise. Or it may be a trap in which the partner wants your work but does not want to provide you with client credit by elevating you to partner. Or the partner may have greater or lesser credibility with fellow partners based on prior evaluations.

The partner may feel that he or she has an obligation to promote all associates and be perceived as favorable to associates so that the partner can continue to get work from them. This may be fine for a short term but may not ultimately provide career support for you.

Pay attention to the markups of documents that you have prepared. Find out what it is that the partner changed in your work, and where possible have a discussion with the partner about it. Sometimes the reasons for the changes will be obvious. Sometimes the partner will have possession of extra facts that prompted a change in what you wrote. Sometimes the partner changes will be style points. You should find out if the substance and the way that you organized or articulated the material were acceptable.

WHAT LAW SCHOOL DOES NOT TEACH

Element by Element Compliance with Specific Statutes, Regulations, and Forms

Law school is intent on teaching the general legal principles in order to provide you with the broadest possible base of knowledge on which to develop particular expertise. It is not a deficit in law school that it teaches broadly rather than narrowly; it just has a specific role in legal education, and it cannot possibly get into the level of detail that a specific work environment would require. The job itself will have specific details it requires you to master, and you will learn them there.

You might learn something in law school about general policy considerations that relate to an area of law, without learning the specific statutory language that has been enacted to address the policy goals. Without a specific reason for a law student to learn it, law school will not teach the statutory language itself, nor investigate the nuances or gaps in that language. You might study some court cases that fill in the missing areas, to determine whether an unaddressed statutory area is implicitly filled in by court decisions or treated as a deliberate legislative omission that the court declines to fill in.

Unless you take specific elective courses, you will not get into the minutiae of different regulations that are adopted in order to implement statutes. Similarly, you will not get into the disputes over the details of those regulations, assuming that any formal adjudications of those disputes even exist.

Often practice will consist of learning where to find a relevant government form and how to understand how to fill in that form. That type of practice is not devoted to resolving or addressing a dispute. That is learning the law in order to obtain a permit or stay compliant with a regulatory requirement and learning how to make sure that the filing is accurate and sufficiently complete. If the client is seeking a permit, the filing will need to be sufficient to obtain the desired permit. If the client is making a regulatory filing, the filing will need to be sufficiently detailed to prevent regulatory curative or enforcement actions.

Depending on the subject matter, there may be a well-developed body of law or information available from secondary sources to assist you in understanding the filing and the form. There may be someone in the law firm who has handled the form before and can pass on the "lore" governing the completion of such documents.

Document Preparation

Documents that you prepare for clients will typically have very specific purposes, and the contents of those documents will reflect those purposes. Legal research that you do may not always be incorporated into the documents themselves, but may be used to shape the contents of the documents. For example, a contract will not include a discussion of the law on points relating to enforceability. It will include terms that courts have determined to be enforceable and exclude terms that courts have determined not to be enforceable.

A motion to compel discovery may contain a discussion of relevant standards governing the requirement that a court rule in your client's favor, or it may just contain the discovery demand. In either case, the preparation of the document will be shaped by your research on why the court will be obligated to comply with your demand. The legal memo you prepared on why the court will be obligated to comply may not be used until a dispute develops.

Accordingly, document preparation may reflect the results of your legal research and analysis, but not the research itself.

Document preparation will be an art that you will learn in practice. There will be times when you are going to have to be exacting, specific, and voluminous in what you include in a document. In a contract for a sale of a business, for example, the parties will typically make representations as to the state of their respective businesses. Those representations may include lists of assets or liabilities, details on claims against the business, or information on specific assets. You may be required to attach an inventory listing of assets in order to meet the requirements of that representation. You may have to review scores of contracts to identify if they contain material provisions, as defined under the agreement, or if they permit or prohibit assignment.

There will be other times that you will want to exclude a term or leave a term unaddressed, because the parties may not have agreed among themselves how to address the question or because the matter is theoretical and not cost-effective to negotiate. Sometimes the client will not want to make a representation that it cannot verify. In a motion, you may want to omit information that you know but are saving to introduce at a different stage of the litigation.

Learning the details of which information to put in, when to put it in, where to put it in, and why to put it in at a particular time will be part of your legal education as an associate. These decisions will entail the use of legal judgment, which by and large you will not have developed in the earliest stages of your career. Learning to make these judgments will be similar to learning which facts are material and which are not, and which laws are relevant and which are not.

Communications with Clients

Communications with clients have many complex elements. In addition to being the way by which work gets done, communications with clients can be privileged and subject to important evidentiary restrictions.

Communications can relate to the development of critical factual information, including information that could be deemed admissions by the client to the accuracy of an opponent's characterization of the facts.

Development of legal strategy occurs with the consent of the client. As a business matter, the partner dealing with the client will want to be in a position to set the client's expectations about what the firm can and cannot deliver and what time frame and resources the firm expects in order to deliver it.

All of these matters are outside the scope of a law school curriculum. For all of these reasons, you will not be entrusted with a great deal of client communication during the initial stages of your legal career. The partners you work with will want to have a sense of your judgment and discretion, your ability to stay on point and not to introduce extraneous information, and your ability to keep private the information that the client wants to keep private.

You are, however, likely to be enlisted to work with the client on development of specific factual information. Working directly with a client on understanding the underlying facts of a situation is relatively neutral, and discussions of the facts are not necessarily going to entail the client forming expectations about the direction of a case or the likelihood of success.

Clients Are Usually Not Lawyers

You may have done some tremendous, groundbreaking, and very advantageous legal research for the client. You may have found the exact applicable precedent that fits the nuances of the case for the position the client wants to assert. There may be some incredible fine point of law and narrow distinction that you have located that will benefit the client and that you can hardly wait to discuss.

Unfortunately, while the outcome is relevant to the client, the fine point of law that is used to generate the outcome usually is not. You can have the good, warm feeling of having found the right point, but most of the time you should not bother the client with it.

Clients need to have an understanding of the legal principles that govern their situation, but they cannot be, and should not be expect to be, lawyers for themselves. They need to understand enough about the governing law issues so that they can recognize and communicate the relevant facts to you or recognize that they should tell you a previously undisclosed relevant fact. But a full discussion of the law with the client is typically not necessary or desirable.

If there is a complete legal discussion to be had, the partner should have it with you.

Negotiation

Depending on your work experience prior to law school, you may or may not have significant negotiating experience. Negotiations are typically conducted in multiple contexts, not simply in contract discussions.

Discussions with a client about the work product or the timing of delivery are negotiations. Discussions with the partner about when you can deliver the product for the client are negotiations. Discussions with your secretary over whether your work or another attorney's work gets done first are negotiations.

Negotiations will include discussing with opposing counsel what will and will not be the timing for the deposition, what can and cannot be asked in deposition, or working on the timing for a status conference with the court. Negotiation skills are typically not taught in law school.

An important reference text for negotiations is the book *Getting to Yes* by Roger Fisher, William Ury, and Bruce Patten (1981). The book, which is brief, to the point, and an excellent introduction to the topic of negotiation, discusses how to negotiate on a principled basis that takes into account the interests of each party to the negotiation.

Negotiating is not the same, exactly, as haggling over positions. There are many attorneys and clients who will want to start a negotiation at position 10, knowing that over time they intend to wind up at position 6, while trading away concessions as they deal with the other side.

The negotiating process is, in a sense, what economists call price discovery. The way that a market finds a price is through a series of signals from multiple buyers and sellers that ultimately result in the discovery of a price point that is an equilibrium point at which business can be done by most buyers and most sellers. Negotiation is price discovery conducted on an individualized basis.

You are not going to be asked to negotiate an entire contract by yourself. You may be asked to work on specific clauses to get used to the give and take involved in the negotiating process.

What you will learn about negotiations is that not all benefits that the client seeks are denominated in dollars. One attorney I know was asked as a first-year associate to negotiate a clause in a settlement agreement relating to the timing of payment. The parties in litigation had reached agreement on settlement terms, but the antagonism that gave rise to the litigation was not abated. Whether the transfer of funds took place before or after 2 P.M. was a matter of a day's bank interest on the money, a matter of a few hundred dollars. Negotiating the outcome with the other side would cost more in attorney's fees than would be gained in interest, going in either direction. "Gee," said the client, "when you put it that way, we aren't really negotiating over something that is about an economic matter. But fighting over the timing would really be more a matter of spite, wouldn't it?" "Exactly," said the attorney, pleased that the client had grasped the point so adroitly. "Good," said the client. "Keep negotiating."

Presenting Legal and Factual Issues to Nonattorneys

There will be different times in which you need to present legal issues or factual issues to nonattorneys. You need to develop presentation skills to communicate clearly and effectively. These skills will include organizing the material in order to make an effective presentation and then delivering it crisply and accurately.

Outlining is the easiest way to make sure that you have thought of all of the subject matter that you will need to cover in the presentation. By starting with the key topic points, and then redoing the outline to include increasing levels of detail under each topic, you will see what it is that you are presenting, the interrelationships of topics with one another, and any gaps in the facts or analysis.

It is faster and easier to start with an outline of key topics and to devote front-end time to refining the outline than to start writing and, after several hours of work, discover that you have a major undeveloped topic that will make or break your presentation.

If you are asked to make an oral presentation or a presentation that uses PowerPoint or a series of slides, you will want to make a detailed outline, understand the full text of your topic, and then work backward from your prepared text to create bullet point summaries of the most salient points. As with any legal writing, the introduction and the conclusion should be written last, once you know what the conclusion actually is and you have run to the ground all the possible exceptions and reasons that the result could be otherwise.

If you are doing a presentation to an audience of nonattorneys, such as clients or expert witnesses, or even just trying to tell a work story to your family at Thanksgiving, you want to lay out the general legal propositions that govern the matter, then talk abut the factual specifics that determine the outcome. A good rule for thinking about whether you are getting your point across is to think about whether the way you have chosen to explain a matter would be clear to your grandparents, assuming they are not themselves attorneys.

Except with a highly sophisticated audience, there is no way in which oversimplifying a presentation will harm you. You will be astonished at how complicated everything seems to people who are not as deeply involved in the matter as you are.

Assume Responsibility for Everything

Part of working in a law firm is learning how to deliver results. The results may be delivery of signature pages on time, preparing a clause to a contract, doing a research memo, or bringing copies to a conference room while the conference is still going on. The deliverable may be exotic and require full exercise of your intellectual and creative capacities, or it may be mundane and an insult to the amount of money you paid for law school tuition. It does not matter. At the moment that item needs to be delivered, and you are the one tasked with delivering it—that is your job, and any failure to deliver is your problem.

Moreover, you should assume responsibility for making sure that nothing stands in the way of you delivering results. That means having the attitude that if you are delivering copies and there is a sudden electric outage and the copiers don't work, it is your job to find out how to get the copies from a backup system, not to report that it just didn't happen.

Unfair responsibility and accountability are the hallmarks of law practice. Very simply, a client seeks your assistance to obtain results; the only reason the client has any interest in the reasons you failed to deliver on time is that the client is evaluating whether the lack of resources you displayed is endemic to your practice and whether the client should switch law firms.

Presume That the Partner Is Right

I am going to advance the unstartling proposition that you should make a presumption that the partner you are working for is always right.

There are two reasons for this. First, you would be surprised how often partners actually know what they are talking about, even if they fail to have an immediate knowledge of the details and nuances in a narrow point of law that you just spent 20 hours mastering and researching.

It can be frustrating to have your intricate knowledge of a comprehensive case law precedent turned into a side matter and reduced to a bullet point by the partner. On the other hand, the partner will have practiced in the area of law for a significant period of time and has possession of facts about the client and the client's circumstances that you may not have, so the partner can have a different understanding of the context into which your brilliant research has been delivered.

Even if a partner has asked for a document far ahead of the time it is needed and provides no feedback to you about it, or determines that the document is not needed after all, you are better off presuming that the partner needs the document within the time frame that he has requested it, and not second guess what the client's need is. After all, Murphy's Law dictates that the moment you decide that you are working with a partner who sets deadlines by whim and that you are safe in ignoring the deadline will be the moment that the client will come in early and need your work as a critical matter in the case.

The second reason you should presume that the partner knows what he is doing is that it costs you nothing to indulge in that presumption, even if you are wrong. The worst that will happen is that you will have worked too hard, or too fast, or too eagerly, on a matter that had objectively less importance than would correspond to your effort. All that is lost is your effort, and even at that, you will have learned more about your capacity to work hard or work fast.

If you presume that the partner does not know what he is doing and it turns out that you are wrong, you have just made a career choice that involves conducting your practice of law elsewhere.

Good Questions and Good Effort

When you get an assignment, the goal should be to do the assignment. If you ask questions about what the assignment is so that you can obtain relevant facts, purpose of the deliverable, and general understanding of the area of law that will be at issue, those are good questions. You are advancing your understanding of your work, and you are helping the partner who gave you the assignment by making sure that you are working efficiently.

On the other hand, if you ask for step-by-step instruction on what to do, you are decreasing the amount of real assistance that you are providing to the partner who gave you the assignment. At some point, explaining every step to an associate winds up being less efficient for the partner than simply executing the steps that the partner already knows how to do.

You cannot be left with so little instruction as to be completely at sea. That does not teach you anything. If you find yourself feeling completely at a loss for how to do a project, then you should return to the person who assigned the project, describe what it is that you think you should be doing, and find out if you are on the right track. If you are on the wrong track, the partner can use the information on what it is that you have been doing to correct your misimpressions about what was required and reset the direction for you. If you are on the right track, you may still feel at sea and uncomfortable, but at least you will know that you are getting the job done.

In addition to making yourself useful to the partner, the other reason to struggle with the question as best you can is that you learn something from the struggle. Trying to work out how to do something forces you to engage with the question. You learn the structure of the law, and as you grope for a way to fit the facts into a legal matrix, you will learn more about the structure of the law by testing it against those facts, even if you misassemble the critical parts of the law.

Similarly, if you are completing a form, such as a motion or a registration statement, and you try to make sense of the thing that you are being asked to do, you will begin to develop familiarity with the structure of those kinds of documents that will serve you in good stead in future work.

Status Reports

Keep the partner apprised of your progress. This does not mean providing excruciating interim details of an incomplete process or giving the partner an uninformed judgment. It does mean letting the partner know the number of hours spent or cases read or the state of the drafting and letting the partner know if you think you are still on deadline or whether you are likely to exceed the time allowed for the deadline.

Providing the partner with feedback on progress means that if you are in trouble on a document that is in the critical path on a project, the partner has time to make additional preparations. If you deliver an incomplete draft at the last minute or late, and significant work is still required on the document but the partner has not been able to allocate time to work on it, you will have put the partner in danger of failing to deliver to the client. The partner is responsible for taking all the steps to ensure that you deliver your work product on time, but if you let the assigning partner down, the problem the partner has with a disappointed client will become your problem.

Partners Are Not Your Friends

Law firm partners are often warm, genuine people who possess thoughts and emotions like those of real people, or even associates. Partners can have a concern for your career and for your development. They can work with you to ensure that you become a well-developed attorney.

That said, they are not your pals. You should develop good relationships with all partners at the firm. You should work to ensure that they have a sense of who you are—of the human being behind the statistics that the partners see in the firm production reports.

Nonetheless, however interested in your development any partners are, they will always be under a constraint. You may have to be fired someday. There is an assumption that you won't be, but even associates who are strong candidates for partner can have a bad year.

Recognizing the Scope of Your Authority

When you are given an assignment, that is the matter you should be working on. There are a couple of circumstances in which you may be tempted to go outside the scope of the project assigned: when the project looks like it is wrong and when there is something that seems like a natural extension of the issue or document that you are working on.

If something looks wrong to you, address it immediately with the partner. You may have misunderstood what you were assigned, in which case you should correct the information as quickly as possible and get on the right track. It is possible that you have identified a problem and the need to correct it is immediate, particularly if other documents or decisions hinge on the resolution of the question you are working on.

If you think something is wrong, you should double-check your work. You will get credit for spotting a real problem, but run the risk of being deemed Chicken Little if you spot a problem that a more thorough review would have demonstrated was not a problem at all.

You might see something that is a natural extension of the question that you have been asked. By all means take initiative and be enthusiastic. If you think there is a natural follow-on, tell the partner and explain why you think it will be relevant and useful to do the additional work. The dialogue will help the partner understand your thinking and analytical process and, assuming that you are correct, it will enhance the partner's understanding of why you are a good associate to work with.

Letter and Email Writing

All communications—even a letter saying no more than "enclosed please find the following documents"—need to be free from typographical and syntactical errors. Obvious errors interfere and detract from the message you are sending. Letters with errors also permit the client to form the impression that you are not sufficiently attentive to detail. The issue here is not that letters without typos will impress a client; rather, letters with typos can leave an unfavorable impression.

Letters should be organized, professional in tone, and clear. If there are separate topics being addressed in the letter, provide subheadings or number the topics as a guide to the reader.

Emails should follow the same rules as letters.

Don't Assume Someone Read Your Email Just Because You Sent It

Just because you sent an email doesn't mean that the partner read it. Or even if the partner read it, it doesn't mean the partner has acted on it. You have the responsibility to make sure that your work has been successfully completed.

If you are communicating to a partner, make sure you get confirmation that your communication has been received, and if there were follow-up matters, make sure they are covered in the communication before you call the communication complete.

Partners can be busy, and they can be distracted by other clients. If you take responsibility for ensuring that communications are complete, you are helping the partner by making sure that there are no points left open.

Voicemail

When you leave voicemails, leave the recipient's information on how to get back to you, unless you do not want them to get back to you.

Voicemail can be an ally in your day-to-day work. If you have work that needs to be done on deadline, you can avoid distraction by letting messages roll over into voicemail—assuming that you check from time to time to make sure that your spouse was not calling from the freeway with a flat tire.

Voicemail can be a way of avoiding the issues that might arise when the party on the other side asks when the brief will be coming. It can be a way of avoiding direct interaction and questions and answers that might arise if a partner wants to know when a slow-moving project is coming.

It is a tool to be used wisely. Answer voicemails. Answer them the same day if possible. Some attorneys adopt a two-hour response rule to make sure that they are being responsive. You should meet or exceed the practices of your firm, if the firm has adopted any. If every other attorney in the firm is responding to clients within 15 minutes of receiving a voicemail, then you should provide the level of service the client has come to expect.

You should not assume that simply because you have left a voicemail that the other party has received it, or listened to it all the way through, or understands the message you left. As with email, a voicemail communication is not complete until you have gotten verification that the voicemail you left has been received and accurately understood.

Organization Skills

You have to be organized in order to conduct the practice of law. Organization will take many shapes, including organizing your time, organizing the internal structure of documents you prepare, and organizing files.

You have to track tasks and not let deadlines slip by. Many activities will monitor themselves, in the sense that you will be hounded by partners or clients for the work product and will not have a chance to let delivery of a product slip.

However, there will be many times in which you are the person who knows best what the key topics are, and no one else will monitor them for you. If you have not covered all of the necessary topics, it may be an error that no one will notice other than the attorney on the other side of the matter, who may (in an adversarial proceeding) exploit your oversight.

You have to be able to get your hands on documents quickly. Electronic filing of emails and documents makes searching and locating some documents easy, but hard copy documents with signatures can be critical to have at hand as well, and to organize those requires filing assistance.

You have to have internal organization of your documents. You need to outline, outline, and outline again, and then write once you know that the form of your argument or narrative proceeds clearly and consistently.

Political Skills

You are not submitting papers anonymously for grading in a law firm; you are working in an environment in which the core mission is the delivery of legal services to clients. But interpersonal issues among the partners can affect the interactions.

As an associate, you should not look for opportunities to involve yourself in office politics. Involvement in office politics presents a chance to make enemies as well as friends, and as a junior attorney, you are expendable. You should, however, try to be attuned to the nature of the office politics and use that awareness to steer clear of potential areas of controversy where possible.

Use of Technology

Most attorneys work directly with computers, although some will still prepare written materials longhand or by dictation. The greater the number of tools that you can use, the more likely you are to be in a position to make yourself useful.

PowerPoint and Excel are worth learning, at least at a rudimentary level, in order to be able to make presentations or to make basic calculations. As noted earlier, one useful function of preparing a presentation is that it forces you to boil your discussion points down to a very concise set of words and concepts, letting you test the substance of your presentation.

Excel can be used to sort data and make calculations. Frequently, organizing information in a form that permits you to sort it according to different attributes (alphabetical, location, highest number to lowest) will permit you to discover patterns in the information that were not obvious in the original form.

For calculating financial arrangements, Excel permits testing of different scenarios and allows calculations of interrelated variables. Being in a position to test the impact on multiple variables arising from the change of a key variable will provide you with insight into the nature of many transactions, and it will improve your understanding of the economic impact of key decisions.

Writing Skills

You will be required to write voluminously.

If you can't write, learn.

If you can't learn, do something else other than practicing law.

Timeliness and Need to Meet Deadlines

Deadlines are important to partners. Deadlines are important to clients. You need to have the ability to meet deadlines, and you have to have the ability to recognize if you are working with a project that is in danger of missing a deadline so that you can enlist additional help.

You may not be privy to all of the reasons that a deadline has been set. You may have the experience of delivering something within the deadline for the assigning partner, and then having it sit on that partner's desk. Your job, unfortunately, is not to make the partner responsible to you (although the partner should not set unreasonable or unnecessary deadlines). Your job is to make sure that what you deliver to the partner is delivered on time with the most complete expression of the necessary information.

Courts set deadlines. You need to respect the court deadlines, as your client may be disadvantaged if you do not make the filing on time. Sometimes the courts or opposing counsel will grant extensions of time. Sometimes extensions of time are used as delaying tactics or negotiation tactics to bring pressure to bear on the other party. As an associate, you will not be involved in the extension or manipulation of court deadlines. Your job will require you to provide the necessary material to the partner in sufficient time for the partner to review it prior to the deadline to make sure that the court gets the best possible product.

In negotiations, deadlines can be critical to getting a deal done. One party may be working under critical timing issues driven by regulatory concerns, the timing of obtaining financing, or other matters that are external to the interaction of the buyer and seller.

The reason for the deadline is not necessarily critical, but the ability to respond to it and deliver work product in a timely manner is.

When Is That Assignment Due?

Did the partner not make the deadline clear? Or did the partner tell you and you forgot? Find out. There is no great shame in double-checking the deadline, but vast shame will accrue for missing it.

Proofreading Skills

Beyond typos, you need to be able to recognize where there are substantive errors or errors of form, such as citation problems. You need to be able to read a document for content, with fresh eyes. This can be a very difficult skill to develop, particularly if you are working extensively with a document. Sometimes a document can be so familiar to you that you will overlook missing words, because you know what the document is supposed to say.

Capitalization Tables

If you are in a law firm, you are likely to work with a corporate client. You may be working with issues that do not require you to understand the capital structure of the corporation, such as a labor dispute or a contract claim. Nonetheless, even areas of law that may seem to be far afield from corporate law can be affected by the company capital structure. Option plans that play a part in executive compensation may be governed by the corporate capital structure. The need to make disclosures on environmental or litigation claims may be affected by the company's SEC or bank covenant reporting requirements.

Depending on the specific area of practice, you will learn the differences between common stock and preferred stock, debt and equity, and the other building blocks of a corporate capital structure. Substantive knowledge on corporate capital structures will be critical to advancing in a business practice.

Financial and Accounting Matters

You may not have studied accounting during your law school or undergraduate student career. Accounting issues will assume significant importance in practice, particularly if you are involved in transactional practices, as the issues in accounting turn out to affect the implementation details of everything from stock options to mergers.

Where accounting issues do not predominate, tax issues may. Because taxes ultimately affect the true cost of a transaction (reflected in the expression that "it's not how much you get, it's how much you keep"), tax issues will dominate the implementation details of transactions.

Other Substantive Technical Elements

You will find that if you are working in an area in which critical decisions are based on scientific measurements and findings, and reported results and the verified results, the technical elements of those reports assume critical value to the way transactions are structured and conducted.

You may not have taken chemistry in college, but if you are in the environmental science field, you may be dealing with issues around the presence of parts per million of pollutants in samples. You will be reviewing the validity and methodology of reports to ensure that there are not weaknesses in the science.

As with accounting and tax issues, there will be a need to achieve a certain lay mastery of technical issues in order to speak the language of clients and senior partners who work in these fields.

Never Lose Sight of the Facts

The legal principles that you work so hard to develop form the framework for your analysis, but any problem you are trying to solve in law will be fact specific. These facts are important to keep in sight at all times during the research you are conducting or in reviewing your analysis.

You need to be aware of which variations on the facts will affect the outcome of the issue you are trying to solve. The client may be convinced that the facts that are most important to the client are the facts that are important to you, but the client does not know the law, and you do.

For example, a client might be angry that he performed on a contract and did not get paid, and in the course of the work the other party spoke angrily with him. The client might find the angry communication important. That anger might even be the driving factor for the client to take the matter to court.

From a point of view of the contract dispute, however, an angry exchange of words may be completely irrelevant. The critical question might be how complete the performance was under the contract, whether the other party prevented performance, or whether there were factors in play that could give the other party a valid defense to payment.

Your job is to develop a complete factual description that will let you make an accurate analysis. A client will have a belief about what the most relevant facts are, but that belief may have been formed without the benefit of the legal analysis that you are conducting. You cannot rely on your client's impression of which facts are the relevant facts.

Be Available

In the modern era, there are plenty of electronic devices that have the capability to track you. There can be times when you are the critical link in the chain of documents, knowledge, or personnel. Make sure that it is possible to locate you.

This does not mean that you are not entitled to a personal life or personal time, or that you need to inject yourself with a GPS tracking chip so that the partners can locate you on a Google map from space.

It does mean letting your assistant know if you are out to lunch so that someone is not wasting time looking for you at noon.

Timekeeping

Bills are some of the most intimate communications between attorneys and clients. They are the communications that ask the client to part with money.

Timekeeping is not any attorney's favorite part of the practice of law and never has been. It does, however, provide you with the opportunity to make sure you have tracked what you have done for the client, and it provides the client with an understanding of what it is you have done to justify being paid.

Clients do not know the entire course of action involved in delivering a legal product, any more than you would know all the ingredients that a chef uses to make a dish or all the steps in its preparation. However, the scope of a project may sometimes include additional factual or legal research, or multiple phone calls or interviews to locate an elusive fact or document. If the time you spent doing that is billed through, you want the client to understand that the two-paragraph memo you prepared really did take three hours to produce and that the client would not want anything less than this complete research.

Chapter 2

How to Be Smart

(What to Do)

YOUR EARLY EXPERIENCE IN a law firm will involve answering questions posed by partners and senior associates. You might find yourself writing a memorandum on the status of a particular point of law, or research into developments in the law relating to a particular industry. You might be asked what the timetable is for a particular filing, how a fee is calculated, or how an agency determines whether an entity is or is not covered by its regulations.

In each case, there is a reason that the question is asked: someone is trying to make a decision on a course of action, and that person is looking to you to provide knowledge on that point.

You might get a question that involves becoming steeped in an area of law and developing an expansive expertise in a particular field, but most of the time the depth of knowledge will not be necessary. The answer to the specific question will be sufficient.

When you are asked a question, your analysis in developing an answer will be important, but the answer should provide assistance to the parties making a decision and not be primarily an exercise in developing academic arguments for a position. Associates sometimes answer questions as if they are preparing a chapter regarding general principles of law for a legal treatise. This tendency can be particularly pronounced in associates recently out of law school who have the most recent exposure to academic analyses and have the greatest fondness for them.

Sometimes the right form of answer is far from academic, it is highly simplified—the kind of explanation that you would give to your parents if they were asking whether to buy a motor home or a snowboard. In these cases, you are expected to lay out in plain English the reasons that one choice or another makes sense, and the complexity of various legal doctrines would not be the issue.

Answering questions is one of the hardest skills to learn as an associate, because it requires determining which facts are the most critical. Often the most critical facts are not obvious to a new attorney, simply because that attorney is not yet experienced in law practice.

Keep in mind that the client (or the partner who asked you the question) is ultimately trying to make a decision. The best assistance you can provide to that decision-making process is the clearest, sharpest, and most accurate information on the question you have been asked, including information that is not what the parties may be hoping to hear. If you provide an accurate and honest assessment that a legal position that a client wants to take is untenable or has a strong chance of losing, you are providing the best service you can.

You are not responsible for foreclosing the client from doing what the client wants—the law and the facts are limiting the client's options. Providing the client with an accurate assessment that his first choice for a course of action has a low likelihood of success can permit the client to reevaluate the options available and pick a new course. If the client's preferred course of action has no chance of success, telling him so is critical.

Even in the light of an unfavorable analysis, the client may decide to go forward and take a course of action that includes risk of adverse future legal consequences, such as in the form of litigation or regulatory scrutiny. In that case, it is a risk the client has elected to take, with full information as to the difficulties. If a client has undertaken a risky course, you as an attorney would prefer the client did so with all available information and of the client's own free will.

HOW TO ANSWER QUESTIONS

Condensed to its essence, this is the process I recommend for an associate to follow in answering questions:

- Understand the question being asked.
- Understand the timeline for the answer.
- Double-check that your understanding of the facts and the area of law that you are being asked to investigate are correct. Sometimes the person asking the question will assume that you know facts or legal issues that you do not.
- Make sure you ask whether you have all the facts necessary to find the answer.
- Once you begin your analysis, determine if there are additional facts that could affect the outcome.
- Check with the person who made the assignment for any additional facts.
- Provide status reports as necessary.
- Expect follow-on questions. Even if you are told that the question has been answered in full, the situation may change or additional facts may come to light that require you to revisit the question.

WHAT YOU NEED TO KNOW (EVERYTHING)

You may get a question that seems obscure and tangential to significant issues faced by clients. In fact, there are never small issues, since any issue can, in a particular circumstance, turn out to be the thread that unravels the client's case.

If a partner asks you a question, it's because the partner doesn't already know the answer. If you are being asked for confirmation that there have been no recent case law developments that change settled law, you are being asked the question because the partner's knowledge does not extend to the most recent developments. At the moment you determine the answer, you know more about that matter than anyone else in your practice area, or perhaps even the firm. You should not ignore the opportunity to become the expert on a particular subject matter.

Some questions get asked over and over. Sometimes they are questions that you would not expect to be likely ones to recur, and yet they do. As you have become the expert within your law firm or within your practice group or local office in those matters, you will find your knowledge in demand. This will be the case even if you are a new associate, as you will be the best source within that part of the organization for the particular knowledge.

Be Prepared

In the presentation of the results of any legal research, you should be prepared to answer any legal question that the partner may ask you about the research. If you have prepared a document, you should be prepared to

answer any question that is posed to you about any portion of the document.

With regard to legal research, you may be asked
questions about your methodology, as a way for the
partner to check whether you have chased all potential
issues to ground. You may be asked about additional
topics that are related to the material you researched,
because the partner may have reason to believe that
those areas could affect the researched areas.

You may be asked about your analysis. You may be
asked to test the analysis of the law against an alternative analysis. You may be asked to test your application of the law to the facts against an alternative legal
approach, or be provided with a different hypothetical
set of facts as a way for the partner to test the boundary
conditions on the legal analysis you have provided.

If you have prepared a document, you may be asked
why a particular clause has been included. You may be
asked how different clauses interact with one another.
You may be asked whether the wording you have chosen
is adequate to cover all situations. You may be asked if
the wording you have chosen is narrow enough to eliminate all unwanted interpretations. You may be asked if
the boilerplate provisions at the end of the document
have been vetted to make sure that they are all still
good law or apply to the transaction at hand.

The more you know about what you have done and
why you have done it, the better position you will be
in to answer those questions effectively. In any written

document that you have prepared, you should know why you put in any particular word. The answer "I was just following the form" is not an adequate answer, because that means you are not in a position to explain the legal impact of a particular element of a document that you wrote.

Even if you do not have perfect answers, you should not provide guesses.

In the end, each question that you are asked by a partner is no different from a question that you could expect a client to ask the partner, and you would want to have an entirely adequate explanation in that circumstance.

Find a Mentor (or Suffer)

There is no science to finding a mentor. There is no formula for doing so.

There is no formal requirement that you seek out or develop a mentor relationship with any partner or senior associate in the firm. There is no formal contractual bond that is established in a mentor relationship. Nonetheless, identifying a partner who is willing to provide you with assistance in legal and nonlegal matters within the firm can be a tremendous help to you in dealing with the new environment of a law firm.

A mentor relationship is not necessarily an exclusive working relationship. There are reasons an exclusive working relationship would typically not be healthy:

- Working with only one partner might be a career dead end for you, as other partners in the firm would not have the level of familiarity with you and your work at the time a partnership decision is made.
- Even in firms in which associates become specialists in extremely narrow practice areas, working with more than one partner means you have a chance to broaden your exposure to legal issues, industries, and approaches to problem solving.
- Industries fall out of favor from time to time—anyone whose industry expertise was development of dot-com companies in the early 2000s can vouch for that—and if you are working solely for a partner whose practice falls on hard times, it could be hard for that partner and fatal for you.
- You do not want to be vulnerable to office politics. Not all partners in a law firm like all of the other partners in the law firm. If your career is linked exclusively to a partner whose star is in eclipse within the firm, your choices within that firm will dwindle as well.

From your point of view, the best mentor relationship would be one in which you did not work exclusively for a particular partner. Yet you should benefit from a relationship with a partner whose practice area is consistent with your career objectives and who has an interest in fostering your improvement as an attorney.

An ideal mentor will be an attorney who is willing and able to provide you with meaningful work in the industry or practice area in which you would like to develop your career. The mentor should himself or herself have expertise in that field and be willing to use the projects on which you work as opportunities to pass that learning on to you.

The mentor should have an interest in your development as an attorney, including making sure that you have adequate training to be a practitioner in a particular area of law. An experienced attorney will understand what a well-trained attorney in a particular area of law should know. Your mentor should be able to provide an evaluation of your work and level of knowledge and should help you identify training within the firm or from the outside to develop the additional knowledge you need to become proficient.

The ideal mentor will also want to provide you with the opportunity to develop responsibility for matters and clients appropriate to your level of development as an attorney. At some point you will develop expertise in handling a particular matter or area of law, and at that point you will be an extremely efficient and profitable producer of legal services.

The mentor has to balance the need to use your skills as an efficient producer with the need to stretch you beyond your comfort zone and move your expertise level and career to the next appropriate level. That could entail having you take on additional related work, supervising the work of others more junior to you, or using the expertise directly with the client rather than working through the partner. A partner who is providing you with mentoring will want you to have additional responsibility and will not merely want you to become an efficient billing machine.

As you move forward in your career, a mentor will help you understand the client development and client interaction elements that are part of practice in your area of law.

A mentor can help you in understanding the culture of the firm and its internal operations and processes. As with any organization, a law firm can have informal or unwritten rules, and those rules are no less binding for not being written. There may be personality clashes or rivalries among partners which are not obvious to you, but which a mentor can help you avoid.

Finally, if there are gaps in your performance as an associate, the mentor can help you to correct them. If the gaps are so serious as to lead to your departure from the firm, a mentor may help with the transition, if only by lending a sympathetic ear.

Developing a mentor relationship with a partner is not a make-or-break career matter for you. Career development without a mentor is harder, but not impossible. If you do not have a mentor, you can still develop expertise and become a fine attorney and have a fine career.

Even with a mentor, you will ultimately become responsible for developing your own practice and your own client relationships which become the basis of your career.

Acknowledge Mistakes and Correct Them

Dealing with mistakes is an extremely important part of learning to be an attorney. You will not be perfect. If you are lucky, you will be part of a team that is able to create a high quality work product that limits imperfections to minute and immaterial matters.

Nonetheless, mistakes will occur, sometimes in the heat of a transaction or in the hurried preparation of an emergency document, and there is only one thing to do. Acknowledge the mistake and fix it.

Acknowledging a mistake can be difficult. It is at a minimum embarrassing. If the mistake is sufficiently serious, it may constitute malpractice and subject the firm to liability.

Acknowledging and correcting mistakes are the right things to do. The handling of mistakes is one way in which the ethical standards of the profession provide support for doing the right thing. You do not want to compound an initial mistake by breaching your professional obligation to tend to the client's best interest by allowing the error to go uncorrected.

If you are an associate and have discovered a mistake in work prepared by the firm, you should do several things. First, confirm that you are accurate in your assessment that a mistake has been made. There may have been a deliberate choice by the client to change terms or change material in a document that you were not privy to, and before determining that the document is in error, you should confirm that you have the complete facts about what the document should say. In the context of being a new associate, checking the facts to make sure you have understood them all correctly will be seen by the partners as careful and good behavior; if you are checking the facts in order to make sure there is not an error in a document, you are performing particularly well.

If you determine that an error does exist, you need to make a judgment about the severity and immediacy of the impact of the error. If the error is contained in documents presented to a court, and the judge is about to rule based on the documents, you will be dealing with an immediate crisis. If there is a period of time when parties are exchanging draft documents prior to another scheduled meeting, then you have time to develop a corrective strategy.

You should determine what the right course should be. At the time that you acknowledge the existence of the problem, you should also have some thoughts about what, if anything, can be done to rectify it. If you have considered multiple alternatives and none seems to be an adequate solution, be ready to review your thinking at the time you describe the problem to the supervising attorney.

Discuss the error with your supervisors, whether they are senior associates or partners. Their experience will help them put the issue into perspective. They will have experienced or heard of a situation in the past that will have some bearing.

Unless directed to do so by the partner, or unless there is some emergency circumstance, you would not typically be expected to deal directly with the client about the problem. The partner will want to control the interaction with the client about the existence of the problem and the approaches that have been developed to deal with it.

In such circumstances, the client is not going to be happy. The partner's greater experience in law practice and longer relationship with the client will be important to deal effectively with the client and to assure her that the problem has been handled. Sometimes the fact that a problem is being addressed by someone with gray hair (real or metaphoric) helps convey the sense of seriousness that the firm has about solving the issue.

Be Respectful without Being Obsequious with Clients and Partners

There is a very difficult road to walk in the professional service business. As the law is a service business, the client will have the right to expect that what he is asking for is what he is going to get. That is the reason the high hourly rates are paid.

There are some times when what the client wants is not available in exactly the form he expected as a legal matter. There can be regulatory, statutory, or innumerable other barriers to doing exactly what the client has requested. In those circumstances, your job is to provide a legally responsible equivalent to what the client has requested (or tell the client if that is impossible). You should also make sure that the client takes the recommended course in order to stay legally protected while getting more or less what he requested. Doing so means establishing your expertise on legal matters and communicating to the client that you respect her wishes and are doing what you can do to implement them, subject to the requirements of law and your ethical obligations as an attorney to follow the law.

It is not always simple to establish with the client a tone that is respectful without being obsequious. You will need to develop a way, consistent with your own personality, to convey that you respect the client's wishes and at the same time cannot sacrifice your independent professional judgments.

In that vein, even though you work for the client and serve at the client's pleasure and direction, you must convey that in the attorney-client relationship, by virtue of your legal training and knowledge, you are the arbiter of what the legal requirements are in any situation. You should also convey that you have an obligation to control the use of the firm's name or reputation in advancing the client's purposes.

Within the firm itself, you should be able to work in an environment in which you are presumed to be intelligent and capable. Law firms tend to have at least a general atmosphere of respect among colleagues and an outward veneer of mutual respect among partners, regardless of the reality.

As an associate, you should not encounter situations in which you are treated in an abusive or demeaning fashion. If you do encounter abusive situations, you should reevaluate your stay in the firm, because the situation will not improve. You may think it will improve or be only situational, but it will not improve. Get out.

What Happens if the Client Does Not Take Your Advice?

As an attorney, you are an advisor to the client, but you are not the principal, and you are not the decision maker for the client.

Your recommendations should carry significant weight, once you have experience, because you will be bringing to bear the experience of hundreds of clients in similar situations and because you will have demonstrated your ability to work in the client's best interest.

If you encounter a client who acts in a willful fashion, deliberately ignoring or distorting your advice, then you may have to consider whether this client really has an interest in wanting to obey the law. At that point, you have to document the actions you are taking to keep the client on the right path. You should memorialize your conversations with the client, including the advice given and the time and setting of the conversation, or you should include the advice in a letter or an email so that a record is created of the advice that you have provided and when you have provided it.

You should also discuss with the partner the kinds of concerns that you have. At some point, if the problem persists, there may be a question about whether the client should continue as a client of the firm.

Dealing with Gray Areas

There are often areas in law in which no clearly correct answer presents itself. Often this means that you have encountered an area in which the parties are free to invent their own solutions in a contract, or in which either side may freely argue to the court or regulatory agency as to the correct outcome.

Other times, there are areas in which there is a bright line as to when a matter is illegal. Short of having facts that fit squarely within the test of what is obviously illegal, there may be arguments or rationales as to why a proposed activity is legal, or at least not illegal. In those circumstances, you will need to be guided by the supervisor and by the client's wishes and ultimately by your own judgment as to the appropriateness of the proposed behavior.

You should not talk yourself into a rationale to authorize a client to undertake an activity that has a remote likelihood of being illegal. There are gray areas in law in which a client can validly elect to take a calculated risk that an activity may or may not generate a legal consequence.

What if Someone Asks You to Violate the Law?

You may be asked at some point in your career to do something that clearly and plainly violates the law. Don't do it.

As an associate, I once encountered a partner at a former firm who asked that I help prepare a legal opinion to a lender that would have falsely provided the lender with assurances that the client could accept the loan and that there were no legal issues standing in the way of the loan. To this day, I recall the chill I felt when he said that he wanted "to get the bank real pregnant with this loan, and then tell them" about the problem.

I was an associate, facing a partner who was highly visible within the firm and who had a considerable reputation as a rainmaker. I was convinced that I was going to have to leave the firm. I knew that I was not going to do what the partner instructed me to do, and there was never a temptation for me to do it. In my case, I was able to find another partner in the firm to help me address the problem. The firm and all the lawyers did the right thing.

You may encounter a similar situation and feel pressured or tempted to follow instructions rather than do what is right. You will be making a major life choice, and you have to choose to do the right thing, even if it is difficult or scary.

Chapter 3

How to Be Stupid

(What Not to Do)

IT IS OFTEN SAID that there are many paths to success. It is equally true that there are many paths to failure, and they are well trod by the naïve, the innocent, the inept, the inattentive, and the incompetent.

Not only this chapter but this entire book is replete with discussions of things not to do. Many of these items sound like they should be blindingly obvious. As an intelligent, highly motivated individual accustomed to high levels of success, your reaction undoubtedly is, "Are there really people in law firms who are that dumb?"

The answer is yes. Your goal is not to be one of them.

This chapter does not list all the ways in which stupidity can manifest itself, but it does discuss some important ones.

Don't Send an Email When You Are Angry

Many people, particularly younger people who have lived their whole lives with email and text messaging as a common mode of communication, treat email like it is a typewritten version of a telephone conversation. Nothing could be more wrong. Consider the following:

- Emails live forever, somewhere. You might think that you deleted the email, but you probably are wrong.
- Emails are writings. They need to be as accurately done as any other type of writing that you do, without typographical errors, without syntax errors, and without nonprofessional language.
- Emails are evidence. You should consider what you want them to be evidence of. You may need to show that you communicated a particular piece of advice to a client, at a particular time. In that case, you will want to have preserved your email record—electronically or in a printout that is in the file—to demonstrate what you told the client and when you told it to the client.
- Irony does not come across in emails. Tone is not available in emails. Jokes in emails are very hard to pull off. It is very possible for an email quip to be taken at face value and be regarded as an insult, or have some other unintended effect. Emails are a terrible place to try to be funny.

- Don't write an email when you are angry, just as you wouldn't make an angry phone call or get into a personal confrontation. If you are angry when you are writing an email, do not send it until you have cooled down and had a chance to evaluate what you have written in a placid state of mind. Many statements that you feel you have to make urgently when you are angry you will find, on reflection, you don't need to make at all. With the passage of time, the chance to reconsider, and the cooling of emotion, you will find a way to communicate your concerns without generating the kind of inflammatory response that you risk by sending an angry email.
- You do not get to take back an email. You don't get to tell someone later that they misunderstood the communication, without running the chance that they will present the email in question and ask you to explain what the term "idiot" was intended to mean in context.
- You do not control the distribution of email. Emails can be easily forwarded to parties other than the person you send the email to, and those parties may have a different, and unfriendly, relationship to you. Every email is potentially going to fall into the hands of someone who has interests that are contrary to yours. You do not want your emails to fall into the possession of someone who uses them to your detriment.

- If you are going to be inflammatory, be prepared to bear the consequences.
- Be careful with attachments to emails. You want to make sure that if you say you are sending a document attached to an email, that you actually attach it and that it is the version of the document that you intended to send.
- Be careful with email addresses. Many emails have an address function that provides a quick fill-in of the address bar, but sometimes the first name of an opponent can be the same as the first name of a client, and you do not want the email intended for the client to go to the other side.
- Do not hit "reply to all" unless you truly intend to send a communication to everyone in the email trail. It may not be in the client's best interest to have everyone who received the initial email to see your response. Moreover, you do not know who received a blind copy of the initial email; unless you have addressed the email yourself only to a selected group, you cannot be certain who else got a copy of the reply.
- Do not hit an "all users" button on the firm's internal email system. There are very few communications that you make that need to go to every person in your law firm. At a minimum, your email to everyone in the firm will be an annoyance; in a worse case, you might find yourself forming an unfavorable impression with

partners and associates to whom you would otherwise be anonymous and unknown. (An associate in my firm once sent an email to everyone in the firm about the way she thought the break room ice machine should be properly used. She had not been widely known outside her department before the email. After the email, she was known outside her department, but for her attitudes toward ice machines and not for the quality of her work.)

This is not a recommendation to be bland, noncommittal, or vague in email communications. Quite the contrary. All communications should be to the point, whether in email or in letters. This is not even a recommendation against the creation of an inflammatory email (if circumstances warrant).

For example, I can think of a case of someone who once compared a law firm's governance group to a cross between the Soviet Politburo and the high school prom committee. (Oh wait. That was me...) Do not be inflammatory unless you are ready to bear the consequences.

It Is Not Your Computer; It Is the Firm's Computer

It is also the firm's network. If you are doing Internet searches in the office, the technical staff has access to everything that you do and to every site that you visit. They can backtrack to find out what you were doing when you were Web surfing, whether it was a trip to eBay to pick up Christmas presents, checking out the sports scores, reading the *Wall Street Journal*, or making a visit to a site that would result in a violation of the firm's policies against creation of a hostile work environment.

Don't do anything on your computer for which you are not ready to be held accountable before the partnership, your spouse, or your mother.

Think Through Correspondence

A famous aphorism is "If I had more time I would write a shorter letter."

There is an art to writing letters in a crisp and organized way. The purpose of correspondence is to provide information in a structured way to the recipient, whether it is the client or an opponent.

Any correspondence, either in hard copy or email, has the prospect of becoming evidence. There are no stray comments and you want to take care with the contents of letters.

As you may recall from your evidence class, statements made out of court by a party that are adverse to that party's interest have a special place in the realm of evidence, known as "party admissions" or "admissions against interest." Under the Federal Rules of Evidence, such a statement is not inadmissible hearsay, but can be offered as evidence against the party making the statement.

You want to take care that any comment you make in correspondence, or make on behalf of a client, does not provide an opponent the opportunity to argue that there has been an admission against interest by the client.

Your letters should be to the point and contain only data that pertains to the issue about which you are communicating. If your correspondence is being prepared in response to a letter from an opponent, you should address any claims asserted by that opponent, if only to note your refusal to discuss them in the letter.

Failure to address an assertion offers an aggressive litigator—which is redundant, as there is no other kind—an opportunity to assert that your silence on any raised matter constituted consent to his assertion. Depending on the context, it may be appropriate to respond in detail to an opponent's letter. If you do not provide a detailed response, to prevent your silence from being seized on as constituting grounds for a dispute, it is worthwhile to state simply that you will not make a point-by-point rebuttal of the earlier letter, but disagree with the assertions generally and expect to address them in the future, if necessary, at an appropriate time and place.

Unless it benefits your client, there is not an obligation to answer an opponent's letter point by point; and in fact, there is rarely merit in being drawn into a letter writing match.

Correspondence should be polite and definite. If there is criticism of the conduct of the other party, phrase it to be clear that it is the conduct which is negative or out of bounds. But no matter what a low, vile, subhuman specimen you face on the other side, there is no need to be personally insulting. For one thing, you never know if you will be in the same position some day. For another, you have an ultimate audience that is always potentially in the wings, a client or a jury, which will form judgments about which attorney is wearing the white hat and which is wearing the black hat. You always want to shape the narrative to your client's interests, and you always want the record to reflect that you are the reasonable party. Flinging insults can cast doubts on your temperament and reasonableness.

Vulgarity has no place in correspondence. There might be a time to include strong language in a direct quote by a third party, regarding a matter that is germane to the issues addressed in the letter. You should not be the utterer of those terms in any written context, even in bantering emails with the client.

Think Through Phone Calls

Phone calls differ in an important way from emails, voicemails, or written communications. They are not written down or recorded in a form that can be used without dispute as evidence of the contents of the communication. The essence of a phone conversation is that it is evanescent and unlike other things in the modern digital world, not available for posterity in recorded form.

Parties to the phone conversation may take notes about the contents of the call at the time the call is made or at some point after. The person who took the notes may transfer those notes to third parties. As a matter of evidence, whether notes on a phone conversation were prepared at the same time as the call and whether such notes are generated in the normal course of business might affect whether those notes have credibility or are admissible.

Notes by either party may be accurate or they may be inaccurate, but unless the parties to the phone call share the notes and confirm their accuracy, there is room for dispute as to what occurred in a phone call.

There does not have to be a nefarious or deceptive reason behind a difference of opinion as to what took place on a phone call. It is just normal human behavior for there to be miscommunications, misunderstandings, or partial understandings in any conversation.

When you are dealing with the question of phone conversations or face-to-face meetings involving your client, you have to work through the potential evidence issues presented by the unreliability of an unwritten communication. Handling these issues is part of your job as an attorney.

When it comes to your own phone calls, you need to be aware of the same limitations on the reliability of a phone conversation. This includes the limitations on your own ability to convey a clear and undisputable message to the other party and the limitations on your ability to be certain that the other party understood what you said exactly as you intended.

You will conduct an overwhelmingly large amount of your practice over the telephone. Telephone conversations are immediate and interactive in ways that all written communications are not. They permit the participants to have an efficient and spontaneous transfer of information or to conduct mutual planning. Unlike written communications, phone calls permit you to listen for intonations, points of emphasis, or other cues that are possible in spoken speech.

You need to consider these facts when you make your own telephone communications. Are you conveying information to another party by your tone of voice or choice of language? Is what you are conveying intended or unintended? Is the content of the communication what you and the client intend to convey? While the other party is not going to be able to put the same kind of reliance on an oral statement as would be the case with a written statement, you want to make sure that you are being as accurate as you can you should stay within the limits of what you and the client have agreed to convey at any given time, and be as forthcoming as is prudent.

It is possible that some attorneys will use the lack of written record to lie or manipulate, and there is no practical or realistic antidote to that. If you think that an attorney you are dealing with is being deceptive or dishonest in dealing with you, you should provide a confirming letter or email setting out what you understood the facts and agreements in a phone conversation to be. By doing so, you effectively convert the oral communication to one that is written and subject to verification and confirmation.

There can be circumstances in which the attorney on the other side is so disreputable or untrustworthy that you would want additional participants as witnesses in the phone conversation, to ensure that there is no opportunity for the other attorney to distort or fabricate the contents of the conversation.

Voicemails

Generally speaking, the warnings that pertain to emails pertain to voicemails, with some additional caveats. For example, unlike emails, voicemails permit you to convey tone, intonation, sarcasm, or other speech-related cues. Just as in a phone call, you want to make sure that any information conveyed by a speech-related cue is conveyed deliberately and in the client's interest.

One particular—and perhaps unique—risk relating to voicemails is that more can be recorded than you recognize or intend. The horror story in this regard is the story of Matthew Gloss, the general counsel of Marvell Semiconductor Inc. With two of his colleagues on the speakerphone, he phoned legal counsel at a rival company, Jasmine Networks Inc. When the call connected to voicemail, Gloss left a message and hit the disconnect button—or so he thought. Unknown to Gloss, the phone did not disconnect and the Jasmine counsel was still recording them as they continued to talk about their litigation strategy on speakerphone. In the litigation that ensued over the phone recording, Jasmine claimed that the conversation related to Marvell's plan to steal Jasmine's trade secrets.

As of 2008, the courts were still working out whether the recorded conversation would be admitted as evidence or whether it constituted an unintended disclosure that did not result in a waiver of the attorney-client privilege.

Regardless of the outcome on the privilege issue, when you record your legal strategy on the voicemail of the other side's attorney, it is hard to make it look like an achievement.

Dealing with Obnoxious Opponents

Not only do the bar associations of the United States not weed out dumb lawyers, they do not weed out nasty lawyers with bad personalities or penchants to misbehave. They also do not weed out dishonest and unethical attorneys who lie, manipulate, and conceal evidence as tactics to win. There are a number of things that need to be done when you confront hard-to-deal-with, unethical, or obnoxious opponents.

First, do not mimic the behavior of someone who engages in ego-driven confrontation for confrontation's sake. Your client's best interest is to get the result that you are seeking. Ego struggles among attorneys on the client's nickel are not making the client any money. Your job is not to one-up the attorney on the other side in a single phone call or single meeting. Those battles mean nothing; getting the result for the client is winning the war.

Second, stay on point. There is sometimes a method to the seeming madness of the other side, which is to distract or disorient an opponent who is willing to be drawn into fights that are not germane to the client's issues. Your job is to do your job, not to be lured into a fight over a nonsubstantive matter.

Finally, you should take note of and make reference in your correspondence to the bad behavior, putting it into the context of the true issues of the matter. Pointing out the distractions and bad behavior is not going to shame the attorney on the other side—you already have a demonstration of that attorney's level of ethics and capacity to be shamed.

It does create a record for your client and for your opponent's client as to why the bill is being driven higher by nonessential issues. If there is a matter that needs to go before the court for sanctions, it is never too early to create a record showing repeated abusive behavior.

You should not count on judges to sanction bad behavior. Sanctions happen, but bad behavior happens more often. You should assume that you are on your own. Judges typically do not get involved in disputes among counsel, but let the workings of counsel get woven into the general battles among the disputants before the court.

Bar associations will not sanction bad behavior. There are some open-and-shut cases that bar associations are willing to take on, such as cases in which an alcoholic attorney embezzles money from the client that the attorney is sleeping with.

Anything that is less clear cut would require a bar association to devote limited resources to engaging in a disciplinary battle with someone who is (a) an attorney and (b) fighting for his professional life. There is every incentive for an attorney facing discipline on a narrowly drawn violation—like say, forgery of a client's name or abusing a client's trust—to force the bar association to prove every allegation.

You should be prepared to face attorneys who will conduct scorched-earth litigation and discovery or who will drag their feet in all transactions or otherwise be as bullying and as abusive of the system as possible. They will create obstacles that your attempts to create goodwill will not overcome.

Such behavior ultimately forces a client to consider paying extra to remove the impediment or to go to litigation. It is not cost-effective for the client on the other side, but a client who takes a bullying attorney is typically not looking for compromise or reasonable results anyway.

Dealing with Underprepared Opponents

You will sometimes deal with attorneys who are (or are pretending that they are) not very smart or not up to speed on the matters at hand, or both. State bars in all states have not succeeded in creating a moron-free environment in the practice of law.

An attorney who is feigning ignorance will be a particular kind of challenge, because then you are dealing with someone who is not going to work in a straightforward manner with you and who is, for whatever reason, trying to drag your legal process out by pretending not to know its requirements. It will be time consuming and frustrating to deal with, particularly if the other side's only goal is delay and you cannot prevent that delay. You can ask the other counsel to put questions in writing, to document his or her alleged ignorance, but absent a court order it is hard to prevent someone from stalling.

An attorney who is in fact not very smart, or one who is not experienced in a field of law in which you are working, will be a different challenge. In this case, terms that are simple and obvious to you will have to be explained to him as to their final reasonableness and why in the ecosystem of the law they are structured the way that they are.

You are educating the other attorney using your client's money. That is not a cheap activity, although it may be cost-effective if you are successful in bringing that attorney around to your way of seeing the world.

After all, at that point, you will have taught him everything he knows, but you didn't necessarily teach him everything that you know.

In law, as with other human activities, there is a vast amount of room for insincere kindness to opponents. If you are on the winning side, you lose nothing by declining to demean your adversaries. If you have the losing argument, you gain nothing by antagonizing them.

Discretion Is Better

If you are communicating with the other side, either in litigation or transactional practice, you are better off not volunteering information. If you don't have to say something about your client, don't say it. If something does not advance the client's interests, set up the next question in deposition, or somewhere down the line turn into something useful, then there is no need to volunteer it.

The other side doesn't need to know, and you never know what information is later going to turn out to be critical for them. Even something seemingly innocuous, like the client's attendance at a baseball game, might be something that the other side finds significant with respect to some timing aspect of the case, for example.

This is not a recommendation to be uncordial or impersonal with opposing counsel. Your willingness to be engaging at a personal level with counsel could result in the formation of a level of interpersonal trust that might ultimately bridge at the attorney level a chasm that exists between your respective clients. But such cordiality should not come at the client's expense.

Dealing with Hard-to-Deal-with Personnel

Sometimes you need to create an internal record for your firm or in connection with the representation of a client who is trying to ignore or distort your advice.

In those cases, you will want to create a file—either in memorandum form or in the form of email correspondence—to establish that there is a recurring pattern of problem behavior and that you noticed the behavior and commented on it and tried to address it. If the problem continues in the future, you can then refer to the record (or if it is an internal law firm personnel matter, produce the record) to show that you have been tracking the behavior for a long time and tried to solve it in the past. It puts you in a stronger position to show that the issues were not yours and that they were longstanding.

For personnel matters, such as secretarial discipline or evaluations of paralegals and associates, such records will be essential.

Don't Create Issues Where They Do Not Exist

Legal creativity is the source of many solutions to seemingly intractable problems. Do not go overboard in finding problems that do not exist or hypothesizing circumstances in which an issue could arise. You want to be thorough in thinking through the legal issues and potential ramifications, but if you become too remote from reality, your advice will not be taken seriously.

In personnel matters, do not inflate conflicts to see issues where they do not exist. You need to work with people in your office.

Spell the Client's Name Right

The client will not know whether you have located the most up-to-date precedent on a legal topic governed by the law for a foreign jurisdiction on a narrow issue of law. The client will know whether you spelled his name right.

The problem with typographical errors in legal materials is that the client does not need to have legal training to find them. This will not accrue to your benefit, and it creates the potential for the client to doubt the thoroughness of your efforts.

A typo is not the end of the world (unless, for example, it is leaving out the word *not* in a sentence such as, "Client A will...pay the expenses of B"). However, you should not take the need to eliminate typos lightly. In a competitive law firm, an associate with known lack of attention to detail might find that differentiating factor to be just enough to lose out to another associate in a competition for top assignments or partnership.

Do Not Be Gratuitous

There is plenty of arrogance in highly intelligent, high-performing attorneys who went to top schools. Don't bring it to bear on subordinates or parties on the other side. If you are by nature a smug, superior, or overbearing person, then by all means you are entitled to exercise your rights to be a horrid example of humanity. Just be aware that if you choose to express this personality in the law firm, it is likely not to reflect well on the firm or the client.

Don't Claim to Have Done Work That You Didn't Do

If you tell a partner that you have done a particular piece of research, only make that statement because it is true.

That seems like an exceptionally obvious statement. Nonetheless, I have dealt with a situation in which an associate made a statement to me that he had researched a particular point of law, and I relayed to the client what this associate had told me were the conclusions of his research. I later learned that not only was the statement as to the nature of the law incorrect, but also that the associate, who at that point had left the firm, had not done any research and he had simply made up the answer. As the associate had already quit, I could not fire him.

Don't Guess

Over time you will develop a body of experience with legal issues, and you will begin to develop instincts about the principles underlying a particular body of law. Those instincts will be valuable in helping you anticipate the kinds of answers that will be likely in that area of law. Such instincts will be helpful in making you an efficient researcher, in that an ability to guess in the right area of the answer can draw you closer to finding confirming precedent that your guess was right (or somewhere near).

As a new associate, you are at a stage of your career in which you do not know most of the law, and you do not have the experience to make a reasonable guess. Moreover, if a partner asks you for an answer to a question and you respond with a guess, you have not helped the partner. The partner can guess just as well as you can, and probably better.

It is fine to offer a suggestion about why you think that an answer would lie in a particular direction—the partner can talk it over with you and then you can do the research to find out if you were right.

Chapter 4

What's Good About Law Firms

(and What's Bad)

I N 2004, THE NALP Foundation for Law Career Research and the American Bar Foundation conducted a survey of associates in large firms and considered their satisfaction with their choices in law firm careers. Across a series of potential sources of satisfaction in the work environment, law firms scored highly. Factors such as job security, intellectual challenge, the opportunity to perform socially useful work, the chance to improve skills, compensation, control over work life, and level of responsibility were given high marks by associates in law firms. Even the lowest rated element surveyed—feedback on performance—was still viewed favorably by associates.

The survey notes that there are two key factors involved in the decisions by major metropolitan firms to hire an associate: the quality of the grades of the prospective candidate and the reputation of the law school.

In addition, summer programs are influential in the selection by law students of which firms to join after law school. Not surprisingly, the schools with the leading reputations tend to be the ones from which the leading firms recruit for summer programs and full-time employment.

This chapter summarizes the good points and bad points of law firms.

THE GOOD

Salary Size

Salaries at the major metropolitan firms tend to be very lucrative. The firms are competing among each other for top talent and sometimes are competing for talent with other parts of the private sector, such as hedge funds or venture capital–backed companies that offer potentially enormous equity returns.

Part of the reason that the major firms can offer such high salaries is that they have clients who are not able to make decisions solely on price, but need to shop for a "brand name." In part, those client decisions to use the services of firms where partners charge in the high three figures per hour (and sometimes north of

$1,000 per hour) are based on the fact that such firms have the experience and resources to bring to bear on even the most complex legal questions, permitting the decision on choice of law firm to be made with relative confidence.

In part, selecting a brand name firm insulates an executive from future criticism if something goes wrong; there is no criticism to be had if an executive chooses an "off-brand" law firm and everything goes right; but if anything goes wrong, the choice of law firm will be second-guessed.

In addition, if work has been routinely handled by one law firm for years, the costs of making a switch to a different firm and bringing a new team of attorneys up to speed on the business, the legal posture, and the personalities at issue may outweigh the perceived benefits.

In 2007, the top 100 law firms listed in the *American Lawyer* included 18 firms with more than 1,000 attorneys per firm. The smallest firm on the list was Watchell, Lipton, Rosen & Katz at 204 attorneys (70 partners). As a result, notwithstanding how competitive the requirements of these firms are, they can absorb the recruitment of hundreds of attorneys per year in order to sustain their employee needs.

Not all leading firms need to be large in order to be highly profitable, have big name clients, or charge high fees. Firms such as Wachtell Lipton or Cahill Gordon have carved out niches for themselves in which they are able to charge top dollar for their services and promise of quality. Such highly profitable smaller firms are exceptions, rather than the norm.

Each year, the megafirms—such as the New York–based firms that represent major financial and operating companies—recruit large numbers of attorneys willing to put in the long hours demanded by those firms.

Regional firms can pay high salaries within their regions, but those salaries tend not to be as high as those offered by the national firms. Unlike national firms that represent national and international clients, regional firms may have clients that are large regional players or that are national accounts that require local representation on specific matters. While the salaries at regional firms will represent a good living within a particular region, they are paying on a scale consistent with the region and not in the league of the national and international firms.

In 2007, the average debt for a student exiting law school was $70,000. The top schools are not significantly more expensive than the schools that do not routinely channel attorneys to the megafirms. This means that there is a relative inequality that is developing in the legal practice, at least in the early years of practice, as associates who go into the megafirms can pay off debt quickly compared to their counterparts at smaller firms or in less remunerative practices.

Salaries Are Immediate

If you decide to start your own practice, there is no one standing by on day one to write a check to pay the rent, the LexisNexis service, or your salary. If you are in solo practice you have to find clients, you have to perform services for them, and you have to wait for the bills to get into the payment pipeline before you can have a cash flow.

Law firms are not unique in providing immediate salary: government jobs have immediate pay too, as do jobs in other segments of the private sector. Given the outlay of capital and the lack of immediate salary, not to mention the lack of opportunity to get feedback on your work from an experienced mentor, starting a solo practice is impractical for nearly all new lawyers.

Established Clients

The getting and keeping of clients is an aspect of law practice that requires a separate set of skills from being a good researcher, having a keen sense of how to structure a legal argument, or knowing how to write a good brief or contract.

Moreover, clients vary in the level of sophistication they bring to understanding legal questions, making decisions based on attorney advice, and willingness to pay legal bills on time. As an associate in a law firm, you will tend to be insulated from all of these factors.

You may deal with the client, but more likely you will do so in the context of obtaining key documents or information in connection with a specific project, rather than in the context of making key strategic decisions on which the client relationship will ultimately depend.

Resources

The Internet has democratized legal research to some degree. Many scholarly articles and secondary sources can be obtained quickly and in full text from Web searching that years ago might have been available only with significant outlay of time and cash. Computerized legal research has developed significantly as well, and many courts and agencies will post their cases or significant rules online.

Written legal resources and written work product are still the lifeblood of every attorney. While these resources are more widely available than before to attorneys who are not inside a law firm, there are other resources that only law firms can provide: experienced fellow attorneys who can bring their own analyses and thoughts to bear on your questions; practitioners who have served as judicial clerks who can offer insights into the likely habits of a particular judge; or attorneys who have served within regulatory agencies who know intimately how the agency looks at a particular question and who have significant expertise from having worked on the specific subject matter before.

In addition, law firms have other resources that are critical to freeing an attorney to concentrate on practicing law. Established personnel departments, malpractice insurance, health plans and retirement plans, and billing departments all involve the firm organizing its business practices with nonlawyers to free the lawyers up for client work. In law firms, partners in effect pool their money to provide a marketing and advertising budget that pays for the client lunches, the getting-to-know-you golf games, and the like.

More Sophisticated Clients

Established firms will have already solved the small and repetitive problems and will be relied upon by clients for the projects that involve more complex issues or applications of the law. As a new attorney, you are not likely to be formulating cutting-edge strategies, but you will be called upon to understand those theories, find supporting precedent or help distinguish unfavorable precedent, or do factual development to verify that the approach can properly be taken. This exposure to legal thinking in complex matters will provide excellent training for you.

Training

Firms need you to learn how to practice law. As is discussed in the balance of this book, the practice of law entails the basic research skills and analytical skills that you developed in law school. But it will also entail the mastery of the preparation of specific types of documents in litigation, in appearances before regulatory bodies, in contracts, or in other transactions.

Law practice also entails evaluating the positions that your client wants to take and considering how best to present those positions in documents, face-to-face negotiations, presentations before a court, or depositions. It will entail learning ways to conduct factual research, through witness testimony and depositions or in the course of conducting transactional due diligence.

Training will require you to deepen your knowledge of substantive law well beyond the basic elements learned in law school. Training will also entail your developing familiarity with substantive topics that are the subject matter of your practice or that are fundamental to your client's operations, such as how financial statements are prepared or how environmental contamination is measured and calculated. Training will occur both in a classroom setting and in the context of projects for clients.

Law school teaches the basic elements of the law. The law school teaching is the foundation and is necessary for practice, but the nature of practice is not merely to read cases and know the holdings in cases. Applying the law to a set of facts unique to the client requires you to craft solutions that are both creative and grounded in the real-world limitations of the client's resources. Learning how to solve problems and embody the solution in a form that is useful to the client is an important part of law firm practice.

Development of Technical Proficiency

In the law firm environment, particularly early in an associate's career, an associate will have work critiqued by an experienced attorney. Having a thick skin will help you to make the most effective use of the feedback you are offered.

Before your work sees the light of day and is delivered to clients, it will be checked to ensure that you have mastered the technical issues and presentation issues as well. If you were not a good proofreader before joining a law firm, you will become one. If you were not organized in your writing habits (unlikely, but possible), you will become more organized.

Simply put, most of your work product will involve a communication to a client, an opponent, or a court, or it will embody the agreement between your client and a third party. That work product should be free of typographic errors, which in the best case will be distracting and in the worst case will alter the intended meaning of the document.

Your work should be organized to permit the reader to follow concepts in a logical order. It should clearly identify the main topics and the way those items will be addressed by the parties. When there are exceptions or qualifications to the main topics, the document should clearly set out what the exceptions are and what it is they are exceptions to.

Career Opportunity

The unique career opportunity provided by a law firm is the chance to become an owner by being accepted into the partnership. While some associates begin with a firm and stay in that firm through the partnership decision, there is more associate mobility and more partner mobility in the modern era than there was in the past. As a result, you may become a partner in a firm, but it may not be the firm you first joined as an associate or even the firm you first joined as a partner. Increasingly, firms have developed structures in which partnership has one or more tiers, with economic and firm management participation varying by tier.

A law firm may also provide a certain credential for associates who do not move into a partnership position, but who go on to teaching or in-house positions, either for clients of the firm itself or for corporations that require the expertise that the associate learned at the firm.

Creativity

There are times when the solution to a legal problem involves the use of thinking creatively or developing an insight that others familiar with the problem have not developed. You can find satisfaction in the problem-solving aspect of the practice.

THE BAD

Long Working Hours

Client deadlines can be set by the court, by regulators, or by the needs of a particular transaction. Your ability to perform against those deadlines will be critical. Even in cases in which your work is not bumping up against a hard deadline established by an external authority, you will be asked to deliver work sooner than the deadline. The partner will need that time in order to evaluate, critique, and if necessary change your work or have you change it, and still deliver the work product to the client on time.

Long Hours Doing Firm Activities

Perhaps you were in a summer program at a firm. There may have been parties, golf outings, rafting trips, dinners out—quite the full summer. While those events may have been fun for you, they were (in addition to being fun) work for the attorneys, who were trying to assess the social skills of a potential new hire. They represent an evening away from family for an attorney, who is trying to make sure that all the seats for the law firm were full at the dinner table. The golf trips were critical introductions to potential clients and referral sources. Moreover, there is a lot of administrative paperwork that you were shielded from as a summer clerk but are not shielded from as an associate. In short, even some of the fun is work.

Pressure

Clients can be demanding and want results on a tight schedule. In addition to performing on deadline, there is the need to perform accurately. Some associates have an appetite for working in pressure situations, and some dislike it. Some partners have the ability to work calmly in pressure situations, and some can become unpleasant to work with when the pressure is on. You are not likely to know until the event actually arises. You need to be sure that your appetite for pressure is equal to the task.

Time Away from Family

Regardless of how humane a law firm sets out to be, there are times when a project will demand long hours. In addition to the pressure to perform, long hours can be a kind of pressure by themselves. You may hear from family members that they are not happy that you are away, adding an additional pressure. The hours can take the form of interrupted vacations, missing planned vacations, or taking cell phone calls that interrupt family activities. Over time you will have the ability to understand when and how to handle the interruptions and when you can safely defer taking the call. Initially, you should expect disruption to your family life from time to time.

Working on Weekends and Holidays

Part of working hard is working evenings, weekends, and holidays. There can be times when the client, a court, or a third party suddenly requires a dramatic and dedicated effort that will entail long hours. It is not the case that you always work all of the time on all of the days off for normal people. But the demands of a given project may require work on some days off, and you should be ready to do so.

Losing

Attorneys tend to have competitive personalities, particularly attorneys involved in litigation. No matter how competitive you are, sometimes you lose and sometimes you win, whether in bargaining, in court, in trial, in motion sessions, or in administrative proceedings. Nobody wins every point every time. Learning to deal with setbacks and handle disappointments is part of the game of conducting legal practice.

Dealing with Client Expectations

You want to keep in mind one overarching rule for clients: no surprises. You may not always be able to deliver, but you should focus on not having your clients be surprised. They should not be surprised by a paper that is suddenly required, or a filing that needs to be made, or (worst) by something that adversely affects the client's litigation or financial position, which you could have told them to expect and they did not see coming.

Chapter 5

Partnership Splits

(Who Gets the Kids)

E LSEWHERE IN THIS BOOK THERE are discussions of the ways that firms grow by bringing in lateral partners. *Lateral partner* is law firm jargon for a partner who becomes part of the firm after having established a career and book of business outside the firm, who joins the firm in the expectation that the business will follow.

There are plenty of reasons that partners move from one firm to another, just as there are plenty of reasons that associates move from one firm to another. As discussed in the industry overview section, partners may perceive that they are going to have a better chance to develop clients in a firm other than the one in which they first made partner. Or they may be lured by compensation schemes that are superior in one firm over another. They may have clients who are moving from one firm to another, and the partner goes along to follow the historic source of work. The reasons can vary.

The new firm may or may not have sufficient resources to meet the new partner's needs. Or the new firm may have plenty of associates, but not in the practice area the lateral partner needs. In that case, the partner may also look to reach back into the old firm to find associates to come along with him.

Associates who like working for a particular partner may have higher loyalty to that partner than to the firm as a whole and may want to go along to the new firm with the lateral partner, if they can.

Law firm partners have fiduciary duties to one another, and poaching associates from the firm that you are departing, in addition to creating hard feelings, may also generate a cause of action, depending on the rules of the local jurisdiction and the relevant terms of the law firm's partnership agreement. This means that partners tend to be careful in the way they approach the situation of hiring any new associates.

On the other hand, sometimes the work for an associate dries up with the departure of a partner, and the firm losing the partner might want to see the associate go as well, for cost and morale reasons.

There are two important things that you should bear in mind if a partner that you are working with goes to another firm:

1. If the partner goes to another firm and recruits you to come along, it is not about you.
2. If the partner goes to another firm and does not recruit you to come along, it is not about you.

The two things really work out to be just one thing: When a partner changes firms, it is about the partner. You might be affected, but it is not about you.

There may be staff who need additional billable work at the new place, so the partner cannot bring former associates over. There may be litigation dynamics at work in the firm from which the partner departed, such that if even one associate goes to the new firm, the litigation will ensue. The lateral partner and the new firm would want to avoid the litigation even more than either of them would want to have a trained associate.

The partner may want to bring you over to the new firm, but then you might be lost in a sea of similar associates there, whereas you would be a star if you remained at the old firm.

Whatever is true about the partner's decision to recruit—or not recruit—any given associate, it is not driven by the quality of the associate. It is driven by the needs of the partner and the needs of the firm the lateral partner is going to.

Chapter 6

Acting Like a Partner

(From Day One)

ALONG THE LINE AS you work as an associate in a law firm, you are likely to hear something about needing to "act like a partner."

This is not an encouragement to the young and untrained to adopt the worst traits or characteristics of partners, such as consuming concern over compensation and relative status within the firm; rather, it is an encouragement for young attorneys to adopt the best attributes of those attorneys who became partners. They became partners because they demonstrated not only legal acumen but also business skill, as well as the ability to inspire personal confidence, to organize projects, to direct and motivate personnel, and to persuade opponents to adopt the client's positions.

In certain ways, seeking to act like a partner from an early stage is an unrealistic goal for any young associate. The elements that make an attorney eligible to be a partner in a law firm are elusive, situational, and vary from firm to firm, although there are attributes that are constant. Those attributes include determination to deliver results to clients and the ability to deliver the results in a timely fashion—either by working long hours or by being brutally effective and well organized during the hours worked, or both. These are attributes that an attorney develops from repeated exposure to situations that require prompt response and development of creative solutions. In short, in developing judgment and a set of legal tools that you can command, there is no substitute for experience.

There is no way to gain that experience other than by spending the time that it takes to do so, but you need to put yourself in situations to ensure that you gain the experience. Even as a new associate, there are things you can do that demonstrate partnership-level aptitude without experience and expertise or that improve your chances to get the experience and make use of it. These things demonstrate attributes of character and personality that are consistent with those attributes that partners like to consider as their best.

TAKE OWNERSHIP OF EACH ISSUE

One of the most critical aspects of performing well as a partner will be that you have the ability to be attentive to the requirements of the client. In the initial phases of your career, you should think of the partner who is providing you the work as your client.

When you hear a phrase about taking ownership of a problem, the meaning is that you assume personal responsibility for following through to ensure that the requested results occur. For example, consider the best case and worst case outcomes if you follow through with (what you think is) everything necessary on an assignment, and then ask the partner if everything that needed to be done is done, and done correctly.

In the best case, you may find that there is an additional element or next stage to the project that you have to put yourself in position to perform, to expand your understanding of the project and the subject matter and to become more integral to the particular project.

You may find that the partner is willing to provide you feedback on what was done well or not well on the part of the project you have done. You can use that feedback to improve your future performance.

You will also have demonstrated to that partner that you have a responsible attitude and an appetite for work and for feedback. Those attributes mean that there is an opportunity for you to learn, perhaps at an accelerated pace compared to other associates.

In the worst case, your offer to perform additional work will not be accepted. Unless you have some socially malignant personality or are wrongheadedly persistent so that the partner comes to consider you to be a pest, there is no downside to asking if there is more to do.

By contrast, if you adopt a check-the-box attitude (that if you have turned in something that you were asked to do, you are done), you are not taking ownership of the issue. The best case scenario in taking a check-the-box approach is that your work was terrific, and the partner proactively takes the time to come to you and provide you with insights as to why it was praiseworthy.

Not likely.

Even in a medium case scenario, in which no further work was required, you still missed the chance to get partner feedback, even nonverbal feedback, about how the project went. In the worst case scenario, the partner may have wanted something additional and not have gotten it, and he may have decided to do the work personally rather than try to instruct an indifferent associate.

WEAKNESSES—IDENTIFY
THEM AND OVERCOME THEM

There are areas in which you can improve. You may not spell well. You may have holes in your knowledge of grammar. You may need to improve the organization of arguments. You may not cite cases in the form that the firm prefers. You may not have taken a course in law school that would have given you grounding in an area of law and may need to take a seminar or go through a treatise in order to pick it up.

There are going to be weaknesses in your skill set or knowledge base when you start. You need feedback in order to know where you have the weaknesses that need to be eliminated. Even if your theory is that you don't need to bother improving your weaknesses, if you just improve strengths and dominate on that basis, there is still the need to make sure that your weaknesses do not prevent you from being capable. You have to avoid fatal flaws.

How you overcome a weakness will depend on who you are and what the weakness is. If you have trouble proofreading, then you can usually ask another associate to help you look over a document and look for flaws that you have overlooked, while you improve your skills. You can try reading out loud, as that slows down your reading and the act of pronunciation helps focus your attention on the letters that are actually in front of you. This can be helpful when you know by heart what the text should say and might otherwise skip over an error.

If you have trouble organizing your thoughts in your writing, you may trying improving your outlining process. Go through multiple drafts of outlining in order to strengthen and test your arguments, the sequence of the arguments, and the structure of the arguments.

Ultimately your ticket to getting stronger will be to find someone who can provide feedback to help you identify your weaknesses and someone who can help you review interim drafts of work product to monitor your progress and help you overcome blind spots.

ESCAPE THE LIBRARY

If your only work is research and writing, then you will be gaining great technical proficiency, but you will be missing the chance to develop the other critical side of your skills as an attorney: the personal side of the law. You need to have the chance to deal on the fly with clients and partners to see how their minds work and to see what is driving their behaviors.

The library may be a natural comfort zone for you. There will be plentiful assignments for you to research, and you may have exemplary writing skills that you enjoy showing off. Library research can offer a great deal of attraction for someone who has spent most of his or her life as a student to excel at what is essentially homework. You may need to do research work for a while to get your feet under you when you first join the firm, but you need to move past that in order to progress in your legal career.

Find a chance to go to court or an administrative hearing. Find a chance to sit in on a negotiation session or a drafting session for a public offering. You are adding to your storehouse of experience and expertise when you are in the library, and you are adding to it even more when you expand your repertoire of experience by doing something outside of the library.

WORK IS NOT AN INBOX
ISSUE—GO GET IT

If there is nothing in your inbox, you need to go talk to a partner to put something into your inbox. Firms handle work assignments in individual ways, and there may be a coordinator or practice chair or department chair who is your point of contact for locating assignments. It is also possible that work comes to associates on a catch-as-catch-can basis and you will have too much or too little at any given moment, as a result of individual partners acting independently and without coordination. Even with a coordinator or theoretical work funneling process, you might wind up getting work over the transom from individual partners. The firms have an interest in trying to ensure that work is spread around to get as many attorneys billing as much as possible and to get as many associates trained as possible.

You will invariably end up working more often with one attorney or a small group of attorneys as you develop expertise and a history with an individual client. Some clients wind up being highly demanding on associate time and others do not, and a transaction or piece of litigation can ebb and flow.

Given the workloads associates in major law firms face, making sure to get enough work is not typically the issue. If you are having a slow time—which can happen, particularly during slow times in the economy—you may want to slow down and savor it. The problem, of course, is that if the slowdown persists, your hours are down, and you may find that you are on the list of the less busy associates who are asked to justify their existence in the firm. If you do get into a slow period, find partners who will work with you to keep the time up.

If you find you are not getting work that you want or that the work you are getting is taking your career in a direction you don't like, don't slough through the work you have. Just go out and find the partners who will give you the work you want.

CLOSE OUT ISSUES AND PROJECTS

Sometimes associates are afraid to bring a project to a close. Sometimes there is the uncertainty of what happens next if the project is done, or there is a perfectionist streak that says not every item is tied in, or there is some other reason for not bringing matters to a close. Don't be satisfied with incremental steps. Bring the matter to a close.

Deadlines are very useful as ways to bring finality to a project. When there is a deadline, a project is finished at deadline, not because it has been done perfectly, but because it has been done the best it can be within the time allotted. There is a chance that the work that you are doing is the missing link in a chain of work on a project and that someone else will be unable to start until you finish. You do not want to hold up progress. Finish.

Sometimes the key to finishing is getting a party on the other side of the litigation or the transaction to make a decision. That is a factor that is not in your control in the same way that finishing your own work is.

You will need to develop experience in order to learn the art of setting agreements, deadlines, and expectations for the other side. You will also need experience to know how to cajole, shame, or badger the other side into finishing up their side of the deal. The best method will arise out of the individual circumstances of the case. Sometimes the attorney on the other side is not moving fast enough, and you have to ask your client to work with the principal on the other side to get the other attorney moving. Sometimes you have to tell the other attorney that you are going to recommend to the client that it is time to walk away from the table and that all negotiations have ended, as a way to generate a final decision. The approach that does not generate a result is the approach of phoning the other lawyer, leaving a voicemail, and then telling the client that the other side is being slow.

If you have in mind that your goal is to reach resolution on a matter and not just to push the ball around the field and bill a little time on it each day, you will force yourself to develop approaches to getting matters closed.

DON'T WAIT FOR FEEDBACK, SEEK IT OUT

Partners will be quite busy delivering client work, preparing for additional work, reviewing the work of associates, working on firm matters, or otherwise being occupied with matters for which your work may represent only a small contribution. Partners should provide feedback to associates in order to promote their growth and in order to make them better contributors to the firm, the partner, and the client. But sometimes life gets in the way.

The desirability of providing feedback to associates may take second place to other activities that preoccupy the partner. In that case, you may get feedback on your work long after the fact or not at all, and you may lose the opportunity to learn from what was done correctly or incorrectly while the details of the project are fresh in your mind. You can improve your odds of getting feedback if you ask for it.

If you seek out feedback, you take the initiative and force the partner to either provide you with feedback or put you off. If you are put off the first time you ask, it increases the pressure on the partner to provide feedback the next time you ask. Sooner or later, you will get the feedback that you are after. Otherwise, you are leaving the issue of the feedback that can improve your performance to the whim of the partner, who might not be willing to make you a priority.

Following are a few words about feedback:

- Feedback is a gift. Feedback comes from partners, clients, and fellow associates and staff. Each person has an individual communication style, and the variety of communication styles that you encounter will require you to be flexible so that you can hear the feedback accurately.

Feedback takes a variety of forms. One is the direct praise or condemnation of a project at the time you finish it. That kind of feedback might be vague and encouraging—"this is great"— or it might be vague and discouraging—"this stinks"—or the feedback could be detailed.

Another form of feedback is the continued delivery of work to your door or the disappearance of work from your door, by any given partner or a number of partners. Sometimes it depends on where you physically maintain your office— if you are out of sight, you may be out of mind.

You will get an annual review, which may include specific comments about specific projects or strengths and weaknesses as perceived by the partners and senior associates. And of course, there is finally the sincerest form of feedback: bonuses and compensation increases. It is the most sincere and least informative.

- You can be proactive in telling partners how you want to get feedback.

If you encourage feedback, then you not only increase the likelihood of getting it—and in the time frame that you want—you can have a dialogue about what is working for you and not working for you in the feedback process.

You may want a level of specificity in follow-on advice that is not part of the firm's standard annual review process. You may have questions on a particular project, such as how decisions were made that ran contrary to what you expected. If the partner's way of giving you feedback is not helpful to you in providing him with product that he likes, see if there is a way to make sure that you and the partner see eye to eye at the time of the feedback so there can be a better product next time.

- Have thick skin. You are going to hear something negative in your review, and you are going to feel terrible. You are going to encounter a situation in which, literally, missing a comma affects the meaning of a document, and you were in a position to prevent the problem and didn't, and you are going to take it to heart. And if you do not take it to heart, you are probably a malpractice risk for the firm.

  Someone is going to call you on the things you can do better. Some folks want you to do better and will tell you how to get better in a way that makes you want to perform for them and succeed just to meet their expectations. Other folks will tell you that excellence is the expectation, that any deviation from excellence is a problem, and that the problem is yours to solve.

No one likes to get news about things that they did not do well or perfectly. And very often on the partner's side, there is a reluctance to be the bearer of bad news. So sometimes there is no feedback or limited feedback because the partner has a problem delivering even constructive criticism or delivering negative news in a way that does not turn into hostility and accusation.

Moreover, just because you know you deserve to be fired doesn't mean that you will be.

It hurts. Take it, learn from it. Move on.

- Hear feedback in the spirit intended. If the firm hates you, you will be fired, unless you control a key account. So if you are getting an uncomfortable and unhappy review and you are not being fired, you are being told to get better. So you should get better. The review will be specific about what you should do. Figure out how to get better at whatever it is you need to.

  The intended spirit is to improve the performance you bring to the firm's projects. People do learn and do get better, and if you have a weakness—and you will—then use the review process to find the weakness and improve your skills.

- The feedback is not always really patronizing. When you get feedback you may feel like the partner is treating you like you are stupid. For the moment, let's set aside the question of whether, as a new associate, you really are stupid in the ways that matter to the project at hand.

You may think that a partner is being patronizing when he or she wants to explain again and again or to explain in detail a particular project. You might be someone who gets things by implication; you might be two steps ahead as the explanation is delivered. If you are and if you are right, that is terrific.

Bear with the explanation. Demonstrate your knowledge by repeating back accurately to the partner what you understand so that he or she knows you are smart enough to get it the first time. However, do not assume that you got it all by implication—because you might be wrong. You do not want to be impatient with a partner for providing you all the relevant facts, and then be in such a hurry to get going that you do something wrong. Then your impatience with a long-winded explanation turns into a fault in you, one that might cost the client or the project time and money.

You are more likely to have matters underexplained rather than overexplained; but in either case, the reason for a partner providing you with an imperfect explanation will most likely have something to do with the partner, and not with you. If the partner is underexplaining, it is not a question of you being dumb if you don't get it, or that you are seen as having powers of perception that you do not. If the partner is overexplaining, he or she is not necessarily thinking you're a dolt who needs a map to find your anatomy using two hands. Though you should judge this based on prior interactions and whether there was anything that occurred in the past that might have left that impression.

The likeliest explanation is that this is just the way the partner wants to explain it. Roll with it, ask questions as needed, or take the information and run if there is too much information given.

Chapter 7

Balancing Work and Life

("Will Daddy Be Visiting Us for Dinner Tonight?")

A LAW CAREER WILL PLACE large demands on your time and energy. From their differing individual perspectives, law students, law firm associates, and law firm partners are all concerned with the balance of life and work.

Perhaps the best summation was offered by my daughter when she was four. One morning, as we were getting ready for the day, she turned to my wife and said, "Will Daddy be visiting us for dinner tonight?"

When your child thinks you are a visitor, it means that you are spending a lot of time at the office. While my daughter (now grown) and I have a wonderful relationship, it developed despite the time spent at the office.

If you desire to dedicate your entire life and all of your time to a law firm, the firm will gladly take it. The firm may even reciprocate in terms of money and advancement. As time goes on, you will be a favorite of the partners, provided you do not begin stalking the paralegals or begin showing the other socially undesirable traits that flow more or less naturally from a life misspent in an unrelenting pursuit of the law firm's goals.

As you start a career in a law firm, you should prepare yourself to make choices about how to allocate time between your family and friends and the time you spend at the office. The choices will come up in varying situations, but they will come up again and again, and there are going to be plenty of times when the office will win.

The expenditure of time in the office might be justified. The schedule might be very tough on a temporary basis, for a particular rush project. (And hey, maybe you don't really like your kids that much anyway...)

Dealing with the competing demands of work, family, and your own needs is part of the job description for being an attorney in a private law firm.

There is no single way to address the work-life balance question. Every person has unique circumstances and questions in his life. Even in similar life situations, a person with one personality type would pick one solution and another person with a different personality type would pick something else.

In addition, there are ways in which the weight of the work-life balance question falls disproportionately on women rather than on men. While women and men both have an interest in their families, women still do the actual childbearing, necessitating the use of maternity leave. Male attorneys may have paternity leave available to them, but not all take it. Within the law services industry, more women than men use law firm flextime and reduced-time programs.

As an industry, law wants to take advantage of the skills and intelligence of women, rather than exclude half the population from its potential workforce. However, professional and commercial factors limit what firms offer to address work-life balance questions.

ASSOCIATES AND FIRMS BOTH WANT TO FIND SOLUTIONS TO WORK-LIFE BALANCE ISSUES

For firms, work-life balance issues are an element in financial performance. On the one hand, there is work to be done, and on the other hand, firms concerned about their ability to recruit and retain associates want to reduce the extent to which the work environment scares people away.

Associate turnover in law firms is significant. The "After the JD" survey noted that more than one-third of respondents had changed firms at least once (and 18%

had changed firms two or more times) within three years of leaving law school. The turnover is the result of many factors, of which the work-life balance demands are only one.

Law firms pay a lot to recruit associates. They pay for summer associate programs, in which raw, untrained law students are paid salaries equivalent to those of beginning associates, and are wined and dined. They pay headhunter fees of millions of dollars a year to firms to locate and recruit mid-level associates, either as replacements for associates who have left or to fill emerging needs.

Firms then bear the cost of training associates, both in substantive law and in the internal requirements of the individual firm. The training includes conferences, travel, and lodging costs, as well as the cost of internal training and the opportunity cost of placing a demand on associate time that is not then billed out to clients for revenue. In addition, associates who become acquainted with the factual and legal issues for specific clients can then use past exposure to a client to be effective and immediate providers of legal services to those clients.

Retention of associates, up to a point, is cost-effective for firms. It saves the hard-dollar, out-of-pocket costs of recruiting and training; it permits the firm to be a cost-effective provider of services by using trained associates who have exposure to key clients in repeated situations.

Firms do want to weed out the associates who are not good fits for the firm. Performance can be a factor, but other issues, including slowdowns in general economic conditions or within a particular practice area, can also have an impact on how a law firm assesses its needs to retain associates.

In short, from a firm's point of view, its economic self-interest lies in the ability to be in control of the timing and circumstances of an associate's departure. Therefore, the firm has an incentive to provide a work environment that encourages associates to stay until the firm either wants them gone or promoted to partnership or other long-term positions within the firm.

At the same time, associates make choices to leave firms for various reasons. Sometimes the associates are asked to leave and sometimes they want to leave for reasons of their own, such as seeking more satisfying or lucrative work with another firm or in another industry entirely, or to follow a spouse who gets a job or educational opportunity in another city.

LAW FIRM MATH AND WORK-LIFE BALANCE

There are multiple key unavoidable issues that affect the questions of work-life balance:

1. Time is inventory. Law firms sell hours of service. Lawyers are restricted to having 24-hour days like

everyone else. Accordingly, providing an associate with more hours for personal life means less inventory for the firm, all other factors being equal.

Like any other business, a law firm has to balance its revenues and costs to generate profit. In looking forward each year to meeting its obligations to pay rent, salaries to its workforce, professional fees, malpractice insurance, library and LexisNexis fees, court fees, and the myriad costs associated with operating a large business, a law firm will estimate its revenues and costs. Such estimates inevitably translate back into estimates of the hours to be worked by associates and partners for which the clients are billed.

As discussed in the section on the nature of the law firm industry, there are elite firms that raise rates and raise associate salaries as a way of creating barriers to entry to would-be competitors. But outside of that group, most law firms work with a fairly limited number of factors to boost profitability:

- Rates can rise, but only up to the point that the firm's clients (in the aggregate) reduce their purchases of legal services or seek better rates from competitors.
- Expenses can be pared, but at a certain point the firm's bottom-line profits cannot rise without top-line revenue increases.

- More hours can be generated by hiring more associates, but getting more hours from the existing associates will be a cheaper approach, when it can be done.

  Increasing or reducing billable hours represents a relatively controllable variable in the typical law firm business model.

  A large firm may also face additional considerations of not merely whether or when to add additional associates, but where and in what field. A larger firm that has a variety of practice groups may be able to hire associates in one geographic area who can practice in another part of the country or the world. If a large firm needs to decide whether to have 25 ERISA attorneys or only 24, it has the potential to identify work across multiple offices to justify adding the additional attorney.

  In addition to other resources that the megafirms command, the ability to mobilize associates across diverse areas gives them a recruiting edge over smaller or regional firms. That said, once those associates are hired, the firm only makes money by being able to bill out their services.

2. Associates compete, including on the basis of hours billed. Within in the law firm, your performance as an attorney will be measured not only

in absolute terms, but also in relative terms, as the partners compare your performance to that of the other attorneys in the firm. This competition is going to manifest itself in competition for assignments and also in competition for promotional opportunities.

You can be a star litigator. You can argue persuasively, forcefully, and winningly. You can argue in appellate venues and write briefs of logic and poetic brilliance that would bring Oliver Wendell Holmes or Learned Hand to tears. But if the tax nerd in your class year bills 500 more hours than you, he brought a lot more money to the firm.

If you are not working as hard as the other associates you are being compared to, you run the risk that their greater work effort will be the only factor differentiating them from you in the eyes of the partnership.

There are going to be some partners who know you only as an employee number and only in reference to the number of hours that you have billed (and of those hours, you may only be credited with the number that have not been written off as uncollectible).

The larger the firm, the larger the pool of associates in a given class level. That means the odds increase that you will be in a pool that includes a dweeb with no life who is going to set the outer boundary of associate performance, next to whom all other associates will be perceived as slackers.

The good news, if you are a workaholic, is that you will have a leg up in competing with associates who want time for vacations or to watch their children grow.

3. Professionalism is 24/7. You will think about client work at midnight. You will be in a family dinner and have your mind on a client problem. You will be composing legal phrases in the shower.

    As a lawyer, your work will not always be done at your desk. You will have an insight or a question that will pop up in the car as you are commuting. Problems that vex your client will vex you.

    Even if you are not obsessive, you will still find that you often carry your work home with you. If you own a Blackberry or if the firm mandates that you carry one, you will always be accessible to the office. And if you go into litigation, a favorite trick among litigators is to send a motion to the other side late on Friday afternoon, which forces someone to work the weekend.

    Similarly, transactions can take on a life and timing of their own. This can make the principals, attorneys, and accountants who are working on a deal all slaves to a timeline that is designed to make somebody else—typically the party who controls the financing for the transaction—happy.

    Nothing you do in a law firm is likely to rise to the level of the long sleep deprivation on a continuing basis that doctors go through as interns. But your work life will include some very long sleep-deprived nights that will just come with the territory.

In addition to the long hours associated with normal work demands, clients do not always call at your convenience. As a junior attorney, you are less likely to have direct client responsibility of the sort that would make you the point of firm contact in a crisis on a weekend or vacation. On the other hand, if the partner who has primary contact with the client is unavailable and a crisis erupts, you may find yourself being the only person in the firm who possesses sufficient familiarity with a client or a matter to deal with an emergency in its early hours. You might have to identify someone else to do the work—or if it is within the scope of matters that you can competently handle, you may have to do it yourself.

An inconvenience or interruption for you could be a disaster for the client. Even if the client is being alarmist or blowing a problem out of proportion, the client is paying the very significant fees to the firm in the expectation that the firm will address, if not reduce, the client's anxiety. At a minimum, being responsive to the client is a matter of good client relations.

4. Not all valuable time is billable time. The firm will set a minimum-billable-hours target for you.

Depending on the firm, the minimum number may be the real number of billable hours that the firm wants the associates to work, or it may be a lowball number that associates are in fact expected to exceed by hundreds of hours in order to have any real chance at partnership.

As discussed above, the firm sets its budget based on the expectation that associates will work some minimum number of hours of billable time. Between salaries, pro rata allocation of office rent, allocation of the cost of secretarial and other staff support, health benefits, and employer contributions for FICA taxes and retirement plans, the expenses attached to associates can mount up rapidly. It takes a significant number of billable hours that are invoiced and actually collected before the firm starts making money.

But the time that is valuable to the firm is not just the billable time. There are firm events, where you become part of the firm and learn the players and the firm culture. Your attendance at firm parties, lunches, recruiting trips, and the like becomes a part of the time commitment as well.

As your career advances and you are more involved in activities that market the firm and its resources, you are helping to contribute to the firm's revenues. Those types of contributions are also valuable, but alas, not billable either.

Marketing takes time. It is an irreducible requirement to being a successful attorney to have clients, and whether you use writing, or speaking, or networking, or serving on boards as a way to connect to your target market, you will spend some time connecting to that market. You might also get involved in various firm betterment activities, committees, or state bar groups or other activities that are intended to improve the firm, the practice of law, or the community.

In short, from the firm side, maintaining an optimum number of trained personnel on staff and keeping them from burning out means striking a balance between keeping the number of hours worked up and keeping the workforce motivated.

On your side, you will be making the choice between the professional and financial rewards of spending time in the office working on client matters and the personal rewards of spending time with family and friends.

No two people draw the line in the same place, but everybody draws the line.

FULL-TIME PRACTICE, GENDER, AND THE INDUSTRY'S NEED FOR ALTERNATIVES

Part-time and flextime arrangements for working may be less important to a new associate than they are to an established lawyer who is joining the firm laterally or who has been part of the firm and needs to deal with raising children, with an aging parent, or with a family member's long-term medical problem.

Nonetheless, given the number of years until partnership consideration, you should remain aware of these possibilities, because there is some chance that you might need to avail yourself of a part-time or flextime policy over the course of your career. As a new associate, you should think about how the law firm deals with such issues and how that could affect you.

Gender Impacts

Finding ways to provide legal services without requiring the attorneys to work full-time in all cases is not exclusively an issue for women, but it is disproportionately an issue for women. Gender differences exist in the practice of law; women tend to use part-time and flextime arrangements more than men do.

The University of Michigan, one of the nation's leading law schools, conducted a comprehensive survey of its graduates. The men surveyed were more likely than the women to be married, to have a spouse who devoted time to raising children, and to have more children. The men were working about 33 percent longer hours outside the home than the women by 15 years out of law school. By 15 years out of law school, the women were 12 times more likely than the men to have taken time off from paid work for child care, and the women were more likely than the men to have a spouse with a demanding job and higher spousal income.

Such differences, particularly interruptions of the development of a career résumé and development of a client referral network, can affect career options tremendously and affect career choices made by women and men. Women will tend to select practices or industries that permit them to have greater flexibility or predictability in hours, such as working in-house or in government positions. The result associated with such a career choice is to be on a path for lower income. The impact is such that the Michigan survey found a nearly $100,000 pay differential between men and women by 15 years out of law school.

Whether it is a cause or an effect of such choices, women will have lower salaries on average than men, making the opportunity cost of taking a part-time or reduced-time arrangement lower for women than for men.

The survey further noted that such differentials were not so much gender based, as correlated with whether the attorney (male or female) took time off to raise children. To the extent that women's attitudes on child raising or their self-image as parents compel them to focus more on child raising than men do, women bear more of the career and economic costs, even if the pay scale differentials are performance based and not purely gender based.

Alternatives to Practicing Law Full-Time

Firms recognize the economic costs associated with trying to maintain a portion of the firm's workforce as part-time attorneys. Nonetheless, firms recognize the need to have personnel sufficient—and sufficiently motivated—to be responsive to clients on a 24/7 basis. They recognize that the economic costs of reduced-time practice are counterbalanced by the costs that would be associated with having no flexibility and needing to replace trained attorneys or attorneys with significant client relationships. Associates are not simply fungible plug-and-play components who can be easily replaced. Moreover, to the extent that a firm is successful in addressing the daily life issues that its attorneys confront, it creates loyalty and improved morale among its attorneys, which helps the firm succeed.

In the past 20 years, firms have developed partner compensation schemes that are substantially based on the individual contributions of partners to the overall success of the firm. If a partner who is the gateway to a significant client relationship can successfully manage that relationship and the legal work flowing from it while working part-time, the firm does not have an economic incentive to get in the way. In an "eat what you kill" compensation environment, a partner who decides to kill less and eat less does not create the kind of compensation problem that would have arisen under a compensation scheme based solely on seniority.

As discussed in the industry overview portion of this book, such competition for compensation among firms and among partners within a firm is a factor contributing to the extremely strenuous pace of present day legal practice for partners. But it has also made the formerly unthinkable reduced-time legal practice thinkable.

Historically, the answer to whether a law firm would permit part-time work was no. When I began law practice in 1985, my firm handed out a benefits manual that described the maternity leave policy and followed with the comment that "in the history of the firm no man has ever requested paternity leave, nor is it expected that one ever will." (That firm now offers paternity leave.)

Even when firms began to offer part-time policies, an associate (typically female) who used the policy might very well find that her chances to participate in meaningful projects were reduced, that some partners would stop providing her work, that her participation in firm committees was reduced, that she was excluded from projects requiring travel, and that the straight path to partnership had become decidedly more crooked. As a result, being part-time became a badge of second class citizenship compared to which alternative careers quickly became more attractive.

Now, in addition to the incentives firms have to make part-time policies work, technology changes make it possible to conduct meaningful work away from the office. In ways that did not exist a decade ago, email, Internet-based document programs, high-speed data connections, voicemail, and all the other productivity tools that are easily available to attorneys make it possible to work effectively from home and at times after the kids are in bed.

Approaches to providing a flexible schedule might include a shorter work week with reduced billable-hour requirements (and reduced pay), but it could also involve getting time off between assignments, if the practice lends itself toward such an arrangement. It could involve job sharing or having a particular day in which the attorney was not in the office, but was otherwise complying with the full-time requirements.

That said, it does not mean that the work environment in law is now "family friendly" in the way part-time employment in a manufacturing industry might be. In other businesses, production machinery can be stopped or operated by someone else, and products can continue to be produced. In a service industry like law, you are paid well because the skills you bring to the situation are unique; but since they are unique it means only you can bring them.

You cannot step away from your clients for months at a time, and then step back in where you left off. As a partner, you cannot expect your clients to go without legal services simply because you are away from the office. As an associate, a long absence means that you

will find that your work has been reassigned to someone else, and you will be struggling to reestablish yourself and meet your billable-hours requirement when
you return.

This means that regardless of official policies, your
schedule will depend upon you making sure that your
relationships with your partners and your clients with-
stand disruptions in your schedule and that you have
given yourself the tools to be responsive to clients and
partners when you are not in the office. You want to
ensure that you stay current with developments with the
client so that you do not lose time getting up to speed
on the client's situation when you are in the office.

In some cases, firms will require that an attorney
seeking a reduced-time or flexible-time arrangement
work out a formal plan with supervising attorneys or
with management. In this way, both sides can talk
through potential issues, and in the discussion identify
problems for the attorney, the clients, and the firm that
might not have been apparent at first blush. This also
helps establish expectations both on the part of the
firm and the part of the attorney about what will and
will not be part of the part-time arrangement.

What to Look for in Alternative Time Arrangements

Given that associates are competing within a law firm,
the decision to work on anything other than a full-time
basis can have serious career implications. For whatever

reasons in your life, working less than full-time might be the best thing, and so the question is how well the firm will accommodate your choice.

Following are some factors that you should evaluate in the firm's alternative time policies.

Is the policy written?

A written policy indicates that the firm is (a) serious about its interest in providing flexible work arrangements and (b) experienced enough working with part-time situations to have created a written policy. From your perspective as an attorney, you want not only to know whether there is a policy that permits flextime, but whether using that policy is a barrier to future career success.

On the flip side, the lack of a formal written policy could indicate that the firm does not have formal standards to guide users of the policy, but uses ad hoc or political determinants for success. If the success story for the firm's part-time policies was generated by an associate viewed as connected to a powerful partner, then it may raise issues as to the ability of less well-connected associates to achieve a similar level of success.

How does reduced time affect partnership consideration?

The firm should be able to spell out the specific elements in its partnership consideration process that will be affected by use of the reduced-time program. Does it add a year to partnership track? More than a year? How are the variations of full-time partnership track calculated?

If a firm has made partners of attorneys who worked in part-time situations, it is evidence that part-time work is not a barrier to career success. If the firm does not have a history of success, or if there is a history of consistent failure, then the record is not favorable.

How does reduced time affect quality of work assignments?

You should find out, preferably from associates who have used the program, how their work levels and assignment quality were affected by going on reduced-time status.

Also, you should find out whether, or how often, they were forced to resume full-time work roles notwithstanding the part-time status. Were there obstacles, either in the firm or just arising as part of life, that were the product of going to a reduced-time schedule?

What is the impact on pay?

You should expect to be paid less using a reduced-time schedule, but you should find out how much less and whether there are going to be bonuses or other considerations available to you if you exceed expectations for quality or quantity of work, or if you exceed the (reduced) minimum hours requirement.

How are the demands of the part-time arrangement quantified?

The firm should set out what success looks like for someone working on a reduced-time basis, including the hour minimum for both billable hours and non-billable activities.

If the arrangement calls for you to take specified days of the week off, you should make sure you know what will happen if there are court appearances or other work issues that fall on those days. If you work that day, can you take a different day off? Will you have someone who can step in on that project or that day? What happens if you put in extra hours in a day? Will there be a compensating amount of time that you can take?

Is the firm's policy going to give you what you need?
It may turn out that the firm has a flextime policy, but that the flexibility is not enough to meet your needs. In that case, rather than agree to an arrangement that is doomed to fail, you should see if there are ways to get something that meets your specific situation or that can be modified to meet your specific circumstance. If not, you might have to reconcile yourself to working in a situation that is not optimum for your situation or working for as long as you can before you quit or change.

Telecommuting and Travel

The technological capabilities have expanded tremendously in the past decade for attorneys to be effective working remotely. The wide availability of high-speed Internet connections not only makes remote office work possible, it makes remote work highly convenient, and as you sometimes will find when you would rather being doing something else, utterly unavoidable. You will likely be able to shift hours away from the office to the home using telecommuting facilities without too much difficulty. That means that for some, evenings can consist of a dinner with family, followed by a work session after the kids have had bedtime stories, rather than a long day in the office followed by a return to a darkened house in which everyone is asleep. And many firms have videoconferencing capability that is an alternative—not always a great one—to travel. If used properly, these technologies can provide you with a lot of flexibility on time and travel schedules and more time for outside life.

Depending on the firm, you may be able to shift entire days away from the office. However, no matter how convenient and focused computer work done remotely is, you lose the face time and the serendipitous meetings with fellow associates and partners that happen only by being on the scene in the office. Unless you are already a hermit, and the firm likes it that way, you are not going to find that telecommuting works as a full-time method of operating.

On the other hand, for some firms, particularly firms that are international in scope, there may be an opportunity that arises as a result of an overseas posting. International travel, or the chance for extended overseas stays, can be one of the important factors that led you to an international firm. You have probably self-selected to make the commitment of time for such travel.

If you did not join an international firm with the expectation that you would be traveling, you may have to think through what kind of demand a travel schedule might impose on you. Even if you were expecting to do a lot of traveling, you may also find that the opportunity for travel comes up just around the time a chance in romantic or family circumstances has arisen.

As with any of the other work-life balance issues, it will be up to you to draw the line that works for you.

WHAT IF YOU HAVE PROBLEMS?

If you encounter problems with trying to strike a balance between your work and the rest of your life, try to find a friendly ear, either among the associates, who will be experiencing many of the same stresses as you, or with a senior associate or partner, who may be in a position to tell you what happened when he or she had to navigate the same difficulties. In the end, though, it is your work and your life, and it is up to you to balance them.

Law firms can be rewarding places to work, but they can be frustrating for many reasons, including the level of demands that are placed on you. If you allow the frustrations to affect your attitude toward the work or toward coworkers or the firm, you can expect that attitude will show in your work and will affect your success within the firm.

The firm will establish the conditions under which you can achieve career success on its terms. You will have to make the best accommodations that you can to succeed in that environment, but you have to assume responsibility for being the one to make it work. You can change environments by changing firms, and firms do differ; but ultimately, finding a balance in your life is your job and not the firm's job.

Chapter 8

Pay No Attention to That Man Behind the Curtain

(The Legal Industry and How Law Partnerships Work)

T HE MAJORITY OF THIS book is devoted to discussing factors of career success that you can control. It describes how you can act effectively in a law firm environment and what the law firm environment is like so that you can have some context to understand why those recommendations are made.

This section discusses some of the facts about the legal industry that are not in your control, and which will nonetheless be significant determinants in your career success. These industry trends are not strictly in the control of partners or clients either, however much clients may want to see lower legal costs or individual law firm partners might be willing to trade profitability for a less hectic working environment.

This section includes some salary and hourly minimums and similar information that was developed during 2008 or earlier. Even if this specific information becomes outdated by the passage of time, the trend information that is discussed in the section has been developing over decades and will be relevant for many years to come.

LAW FIRMS AND THE AMERICAN LEGAL SERVICES INDUSTRY

Law firms in the United States have been getting bigger for decades. *The American Lawyer* reported in 2007 that its list of the "Am Law 100," the 100 largest American law firms, contained firms whose combined revenues in 2006 were $56.7 billion, an increase over the prior year of 11.4 percent. Here are some more intriguing findings:

- Eleven of those law firms had revenues of $1 billion or more.
- Each of those $1 billion revenue firms had at least 1,000 lawyers, with the smallest being Weil, Gothsal at 1,071 lawyers and the largest being Baker & McKenzie, with 3,082 lawyers.

- During 2006, more than half of the partners of the Am Law 100 realized profits of $1.2 million; partners whose firms who were headquartered in New York realized profits of $2 million.

However they are measured—by revenue, head count, or profitability returned to the partners—these firms can only be described as massive.

As a general rule, the larger the firm, the larger the salary for the associates and the larger the compensation for the partners. Also, as a general rule, the rich firms are getting richer, and there is no reason to think that the trend is not going to continue.

The top segment of the Am Law 100 has been pulling away from the other lower 75 firms in its ability to attract what *The American Lawyer* called the "high-value, price insensitive work" that all law firms desire the most. The firms on this list of the upper end of the upper end tend to be headquartered in New York, but the list also includes some national firms and some litigation specialty firms.

If these firms originally obtained leading positions through the prestige of the academic and career achievement pedigrees of their historic and current personnel, they now use their leadership to extend the lead by offering the most competitive salaries and most socially prestigious work environments.

The winning strategy for these leading firms is to win the salary wars for incoming talent, continue to pass their increased costs to corporate clients who need to show their shareholders that they are using the best law firms, and use the increased profitability to draw lateral partners with equally profitable business, to extend the lead even further.

While the larger firms are increasing their revenue and profitability profiles, there are changes in the way that firms are structured for ownership and control and ultimately, for distribution of the profits they generate. By increasing the number of nonequity partners and decreasing the number of unprofitable partners (de-equitizing partners), the profits for the equity partners that remain increase.

The law firm career path—on which a group of law school graduates joined a firm as new associates, then in constantly decreasing numbers followed to the stages of experienced associate, senior associate, and then to partner—has always been shaped like a funnel, narrowing the further along one went. ("The Elastic Tournament: The Second Big Transformation of the Legal Industry," by Marc S. Galanter and William D. Henderson, 60 *Stanford Law Review*, 102 (April 2008) ("Elastic Tournament"))

In the modern age, not only does the funnel narrow, but there are other stops along the way—such as the counsel position, or nonequity partner, or permanent associate. Even reaching the end of the funnel and reaching partnership does not guarantee tenure.

Of the 2007 Am Law 100, there were only 20 firms that had not adopted a nonequity partnership structure, and among those change was already in the wind.

There are competitive pressures on law firms to adopt such structures. Obviously, the equity partner in a massive firm who can take away a greater and greater portion of the profits of the firm is getting a larger paycheck, and there is economic incentive for that. However, the firm is also in a position to compete for law talent on the basis of profits per partner, so there is incentive to have others come to the firm.

As a result, as an associate entering a law firm, you are facing a tightened competition and trying to get through a narrower door to partnership, but (assuming that you can remain in the partnership) you will make more money. As one research report put it, "equity partnerships have become more profitable than ever, but are much harder to come by and far easier to lose." ("Overview of the Professional Services Industry and the Legal Profession"; a report provided to the Alfred P. Sloan Foundation by the Harvard Law School Center on Lawyers and the Professional Services Industry, by Sean Williams, JD, Research Fellow, and David Nersessian, JD, PhD, Executive Director (2007) ("Sloan Report"))

Within this book there are occasional references to megafirms, a term that is used to describe not just the 11 firms that had 2006 revenues of $1 billion or more, but all of the national and international firms with a business model similar to that of the firms in the Am Law 100. That business model consists of a practice representing primarily large institutional clients; a relatively small number of equity partners; the ability to harness and deploy legal resources in large amounts to handle client problems, if necessary; and an associate-to-partner ratio and minimum associate billing practices that permit partners to capture all of the value of their own work, as well as profit from the work generated by the associates.

As of 2006, firms with 100 or more attorneys comprised about 14 percent of the private practice attorney workforce in the United States. This segment was hiring a disproportionate amount of new law school graduates—about 28 percent of the graduating classes. This is consistent with a 30-year trend of having new law school graduates at least commence their careers in a large firm.

The entry of those new law school graduates into the larger firms is not evenly distributed among law schools: The top 10 law schools, as ranked by *U.S. News & World Report,* represented about 30 percent of the hiring in the top 250 law firms in the country and about 58 percent of the hiring in the top 10 firms in the country.

In other words, if you are a law student and you want to improve your chances to get into a megafirm, you should already have done tremendously on your LSATs and be attending a leading law school. But you already know that.

TRENDS IN THE LEGAL
SERVICES INDUSTRY

No one can predict the course of law firm revenues, billing, or profitability. But there is no reason to think that law firm revenues or profits can grow infinitely. Constraints on the ability to increase rates can take the form of client demands for alternative billing arrangements or choices to take work to other providers who are lower cost for issues that are not the "bet the company" matters. The ability of law firms to generate additional billed hours depends on either getting more work from existing personnel or hiring more attorneys and incurring the associated costs.

Corporate firms increased billing rates by six to eight percent per year from 1995 to 2005. Rate increases are a significant factor in the revenue increases for firms. The other variables that affect revenue increases are increasing the number of hours that associates work or increasing the number of hours partners work, and those have happened as well.

It is possible to increase the number of billed hours by increasing the number of attorneys doing the billing. However, increases in revenues from hiring new attorneys are not translated simply or automatically into income, as the firms are paying increased salaries for associates (starting salaries at leading firms were $160,000 for first-years, not including signing or year-end bonuses).

With regard to hard data on the hours that associates are expected to work, see the report by the National

Association of Law Placement, "How Much Do Associates Have to Work?" *NALP Bulletin*, April 2007.

Getting the existing workforce (both associates and partners) to work more hours is another way to generate more billed time and therefore more revenue. *The Sloan Report* noted, "In the 1960s, associates billed an average of 1,500 hours per year. By 1989 that number had climbed to 1,820. By 2000 it was about 2,100 hours. These trends have continued over the past few years ... Of the largest firms, those over 700 attorneys, 32 percent require associates to bill at least 2,000 hours."

These are not sweatshop-level working conditions. Nationally, the average workweek for associates is about 49 hours of billable work; for the megafirms, the average is 60 hours.

Partners are working harder, too. Between 1985 and 2003, annual billable hours by partners in senior firm positions increased from an average of 1,538 hours to more than 1,700 hours. In part, this is driven by the carrot of firms trying to offer their partners higher incomes by generating higher revenues; in part, this is driven by the stick, in the form of the threat of de-equitization for partners whose profitability compares unfavorably to that of the other partners in their firms.

Clients, as the ones charged the constantly increasing rates, are naturally unhappy and seek alternative billing methods or alternatives to paying high rates. Institutional clients whose purchase of legal services is a repeated and significant annual dollar number have some ability to negotiate on price in ways that intermittent users of legal services do not.

As clients push back on fees, the impact on the law firm may be felt not merely at the top line as a revenue inhibitor. To the extent that the more sophisticated clients demand that a firm use experienced associates, it means that the cost of training new associates is not passed through to clients.

THE RICH GET RICHER (THE TWO-TIER ASSOCIATE SALARY ECONOMY)

As discussed in the prior chapters, the large law firms in the United States represent highly profitable corporate clients that are relatively price-insensitive to the legal fees that those firms charge. The firms, in turn, use associate salaries as a means to recruit top talent to compete with one another, by forcing less profitable law firms to choose between profits and paying top salaries to recruit top talent.

While there is still a diverse group of firms providing legal services across the country, including to the nation's wealthiest corporate clients, the trend has been toward increasing consolidation among law firms for the lucrative corporate legal work. A parallel trend is toward there being two separate economic classes of law firm associates: the ones who went to megafirms and the ones who did not.

As the NALP reported in its January 2008 *NALP Bulletin*, the shape of the graph of the median associate salaries has changed from the early 1990s to the present. In the early 1990s, the graph, like any other bell curve, had a thin left edge (representing exceptionally low salaries), a peak in the middle (representing the distribution of most salaries), and a thin right edge (representing exceptionally high salaries). At that time, the median starting salary for associates was $40,000, with the going rate of $90,000 for the megafirm starting salaries skewing the median salary upward by about $10,000. Now, NALP reports the median salary as being in the range of $62,000, but the graph would be drawn with a two-bell curve distribution. One bell curve is for the starting salaries among the "haves," averaging in a range of $130,000–$150,000, and a second bell curve shows the distribution for the starting salaries among the less economically fortunate associates, averaging in a range nearly $100,000 lower. And there is a relatively smaller distribution of salaries in between the two groups.

At the same time, the *National Law Journal* reported in 2007 that the 250 top law firms that it surveys (the NLJ 250) increasingly took a greater proportion of students from 20 leading law schools. Columbia Law School came in as the top producer of associates for NLJ 250 law firms, with 75 percent of its graduates joining top firms. Northwestern University Law School was second, with 73.5 percent of its graduates joining top firms.

The top 20 schools collectively sent a little more than half of their graduates to NLJ 250 law firms.

It is possible that those statistics somewhat understate the number of graduates from leading schools who join megafirms, since the associates who select judicial clerkships immediately following law school often wind up at major law firms following the clerkship.

Not surprisingly, the credentialing function that the top schools provide—along with the tendency of firms to hire from schools where alumni have become successful attorneys—means that one key to a significant associate salary will be the choice of law school. It is possible to be hired at a large law firm and to succeed at a large law firm without having gone to a top-rated school, but the odds are longer for graduates who did not attend one of the "brand name" schools.

DEBT LOADS FOR NEW ASSOCIATES

One factor that affects new associates is the amount of debt they have accumulated from attending law school. As of 2007, the median debt load among law school graduates surveyed by the NALP was $70,000, with two-thirds of the survey respondents reporting debt levels between $36,000 and $106,000. Law school costs had risen by 267 percent for in-state public law schools between 1990 and 2005, and private law school tuition during that period was up 130 percent.

The debt loads did not correlate to expected legal careers. In other words, associates who went to law firms might command higher salaries than attorneys who went into solo practice or public interest law, and they might have greater ability to service the debt they had incurred in law school. But the career choice did not track the willingness to incur the debt.

THE EVOLVING COMPETITION FOR PROMOTION TO PARTNERSHIP

The ultimate career path in private law firms has traditionally been from associate to partner. The logic of law firm promotion, which has been the traditional structure of law firms for decades, is very simple: a new associate joins the firm, learns the ropes, and does the work the existing partners are too busy to handle themselves, under the supervision of the partners. Over time, the associate would become more proficient, assume greater responsibility, and either join the partnership or, under the "up or out" principle, go elsewhere and be replaced by an incoming crop of new associates.

Over time, the firm would grow, as partners were added at a rate higher than the replacement rate of retiring or dying partners, and the group of associates would increase. This leverage—the use of multiple associates to handle clients who were connected to a single partner or to the firm generally—meant that there was excess value created for the partners to share and that the competition among associates honed their legal skills and their focus on firm matters.

In the most prestigious firms, the "out" part of the "up or out" formula is no small consolation prize. This is because the pedigree and credentialing that the firm provides to someone who was sufficiently skilled and competitive to have joined the firm in the first place provides entrée to other law firms, government positions, in-house positions, or academic positions of significant prestige, financial return, or professional fulfillment. In fact, the alumni association aspects of this arrangement provide reinforcement for the former associates, who become in-house counsel for clients of the firm, to remain as clients of the firm and to funnel new work to the firm.

This arrangement is called the tournament model in academic literature. Like any model, it has elements that are generally effective for describing how the world works, but it is not a perfect description in every case. In the present day, the tournament model has been modified as associates churn in and out of firms at an increasing rate, as partners move in and out of firms, and as intermediate tiers within partnerships have been created, such as nonequity partners, reduced-time partners, of counsel positions, or permanent associate positions.

Moreover, once an aspiring attorney has grabbed the brass ring of partnership, the changes in the way firms compensate partners and the risk that a partner will be de-equitized (that is, turned into an employee rather than an owner of the firm) have meant that attorneys are confronted with the fact that the ring is made out of brass, not gold. Partnership tenure is not forever nor is the compensation of partners assured simply because the attorney has risen through the ranks and been admitted to the club.

In effect, the funnel shape of the classic tournament model—in which large classes of associates were slowly herded toward the narrow door of the partnership through which relatively few would pass—has now been modified so that the funnel, while it still exists, describes only a part of the cycle of promotion, tenure, and compensation in the firm.

In addition, only a portion of the attorneys in the firm are participating in the funneling process. While associates still compete in the tournament, jockeying to become equity partners, the funnel may contain an interim step of being a nonequity partner or junior partner. This creates an additional funnel process with new conditions for becoming full equity partner.

The "up or out" standard has been replaced with the creation of a cadre of legal personnel who are not participants in the tournament. This is either because they are not on a path to become part of the partnership or they have been partners and have been de-equitized as part of the firm's push to enhance its profitability.

Authors Galanter and Henderson describe the tournament as being perpetual, because it not only does not end with the promotion to partnership, but becomes "unending as partners work longer hours, accept differential rewards, and fear de-equitization or early, forced retirement." Their observations about the inner core of partners that own and control the large firms are buttressed by the data from the firms themselves. Nearly one-quarter of the *National Law Journal's* 250 top firms reported a decrease in the number of partners from 2006 to 2007.

There can be many factors at play in such partner decreases, including defections of practice groups and retirements. Another factor that could be in play is the deliberate thinning of the partnership ranks by firms interested in enhancing the profitability of the partners who are left.

In the sports and entertainment industries, a handful of well-known or recognized stars garner rewards that are disproportionately large compared to the rest of the participants in the industry. Similarly, law firms face competitive pressures that force something of a "winner take all" compensation dynamic. Regional markets that could have given rise to regional law firms of power and prestige are being supplanted by national firms, headquartered in New York, which can compete for the best work in those regions and leave what is left to the local firms.

As top dogs in law firms realize that they are in fact on top, they have an enhanced ability to command a bigger share of income, while other contributors take a smaller portion. In negotiating personal compensation, a rainmaking partner who controls key client relationships in a law firm can exploit the fears of the other partners that, in a competitive market, the rainmaker is available to a higher bidder and that other law firms are glad to bid for the rainmaker's services.

Over the past 20 years, there has been a boom in the amount of information available on law firm revenues, partner profitability, and similar financial information on the legal services industry. The information appears in the *National Law Journal, The American Lawyer,* and is available from private consultants as well. This information is in effect a stock quote on the market value of rainmaking partners, and law firms want to make sure they use competitive salaries to retain key partners.

The legal services industry is still significantly fragmented, with literally hundreds of law firm players. It has not consolidated in the same way that the oil industry or even the accounting industry has consolidated. Professional standards that prevent a law firm from representing clients who are adverse to one another should prevent the legal services industry from consolidating as thoroughly as the accounting industry. There is, however, consolidation in the competition for the best work and best paying work.

Such premium work is not simply for "bet the company" questions. Just as any consumer will rely on a known brand to serve as a proxy for locating and analyzing information about competing products, the major law firms with prestige reputations have the ability to obtain work from clients who want to rely on the law firm's brand. The logic of the decision from the client's point of view is that if it buys legal services from a leading law firm and something goes wrong, the client (or to be more specific, the CEO or the general counsel) will not be faulted for the choice of law firm, whatever other issues may emerge. If the client gets services from a firm with a lesser reputation and something goes wrong, there is a chance that the board of directors or shareholders will second-guess that decision after the fact.

Increasing associate salaries are a component of the competition among the leading law firms for top tier work. Not all firms will want to dent their profitability by ratcheting up associate salaries, and only the firms that have clients willing to pay premium bills will be positioned to pass through the increased costs. *The American Lawyer* quotes one commentator who states that there is a "price point [for associate salaries] that not all Am Law 200 firms will be willing to match. We're confident that the number begins with a 2." (As in $200,000.)

Empirical studies of lateral partner movements show that practice areas such as mergers and acquisitions, private equity, white collar crime and securities enforcement, antitrust, and intellectual property command a premium when the partners move to new firms.

Practices in the labor, real estate, public financing, and regulatory areas do not. Galanter and Henderson project that the lateral partner movements among firms that consolidate by practice area will result in the creation of an elite and semi-elite segment in the legal services market. They point to competition in associate salaries as a key element in that trend.

At the same time, some firms are showing signs of dropping out of the pure salary competition, using such strategies as these:

- Following the $160,000 starting associate salary, but moving quickly to a merit pay scale for successive years for associates
- Creating pay differentials within practice areas, with higher pay being provided to associates who work in the more profitable practice areas
- Creating a nonpartnership track tier for which an associate is paid less and is expected to bill less
- Creating an "opt in" compensation scheme that provides higher pay to associates who elect to bill 2,000 or more hours per year or an "opt out" scheme that permits an associate to take a pay cut but work less

The "Elastic Tournament" describes the dilemma the ongoing competition presents for partners. Many partners would gladly exchange lower earnings for a shorter workweek or the opportunity to go on vacation or mentor associates, or in general have a more livable life. And yet no individual partner dares make the choice to step off the treadmill unless all other competing attorneys step off at the same time, for fear of being left behind.

Put differently, whatever the ultimate model of law firm life is, the breaking point beyond which nothing different can be done has still not been reached, and so firms are still aggressively racing to reach it.

Afterword

HOW DO YOU MEASURE SUCCESS?

There is some academic research that demonstrates a correlation between higher profits and unhappy associates. See "Young Associates in Trouble," David T. Zaring and William D. Henderson, *Michigan Law Review*, Vol. 105 (2007). The authors note that "steering associates into highly specialized and repetitive [read: boring] niche practice may be a lucrative management strategy."

There is no reason that outcome should be surprising. Most of what you have to do as a lawyer is hand-crafted and individualized, whether it is for a contract, a brief, or an appearance before an administrative agency. For each client, you are working with the specific facts of a single situation, and even if there are forms and models and precedents that you can work from as a starting point or frame of reference, no case is like any other.

Accordingly, to the extent that a particular area of law does have highly repetitive factual situations, it is possible to create forms that cover most issues with minimal revisions. That makes it possible for the firm to move more toward a business model that looks like a manufacturing plant rather than a craft shop or artisan studio, and the easily reproducible work can be highly profitable.

The good news for associates, though, is that over time unhappy associates represent a cost containment question for the partners.

If associates are unhappy enough, they leave. That creates profitability problems for the partners regarding the cost of recruitment (headhunters cost money, summer clerk programs cost money, signing bonuses cost money, and having a reputation as a sweatshop means needing to pay salaries to offset the negative reputation, which costs money). It also creates profitability problems arising from the cost of training the new recruits, either as to the specifics of the clients or as to the area of law.

Unhappy associates who stay do not create recruitment or training cost questions, but they can create morale or productivity problems.

I am quite sure that if associate misery could be converted reliably into significant additional profitability, law firms would work hard to increase it. But even if unhappy associates are more profitable, there is significant discussion in the legal services industry about finding ways to avoid the costs of churning the associate talent pool and looking for ways to provide associates with job satisfaction.

In the mid-1990s, I served as the general counsel for a publicly traded semiconductor firm. The company made chips that went into communication devices, just as the Internet was taking off. The company was riding a very favorable tide in the market, and it was finally bought out for more than $2 billion.

The engineers who designed the chips for that company were doing cutting-edge work. They had end goals—to use the chips to generate accurate transfers of data, at faster and faster rates. And they had a set of constraints they had to work within—the laws of physics.

In creating these new chips, they were solving problems that no one had ever solved before. To solve those problems, they had to look at the boundaries of the physical laws of the universe and the existing state of technology, and then use creativity and exactitude to come up with an answer.

I loved working with engineers, because their job is just like my job. As a lawyer, you work with statutes, case law, regulations, administrative interpretations, and the occasional arbitrary and capricious ruling from the bench; but in the end, you are trying to achieve a goal for the client, within the constraints imposed by the law.

The work of law can be creative. It can require patience and precision. Sometimes you can see the results immediately, and sometimes you never really know the results. For litigators, it can offer an arena in which to compete. Law practice can offer rewards to practitioners that are measured not merely in dollars.

For that reason, I suggest in the Introduction that you consider how you measure success as a part of your thinking about what it is that you expect or hope you will get from a career in law, which includes practicing in a law firm.

I spend a lot of this book talking about how hard you will work and some of the commonsense ways you can maneuver around a law firm, but I do not talk about why you would want to bother: You can get a sense of achievement. You can obtain status. You can obtain money. You can work on projects that stimulate your intellect or your curiosity, or work for clients whose goals you share and to whose success you will be pleased to contribute. These rewards from the practice of law will sustain you.

I do not dismiss the frustrating times you will encounter; the sacrifices that you, your family, and your friends will bear; or the times that the practice of law (or a particular client or opposing counsel) will seem so awful that going back to school for that MBA degree seems compelling. You are certain to encounter these situations. You are also going to encounter satisfaction, success, and maybe even an occasional sense of triumph.

However you define success and find it, enjoy it.

Index